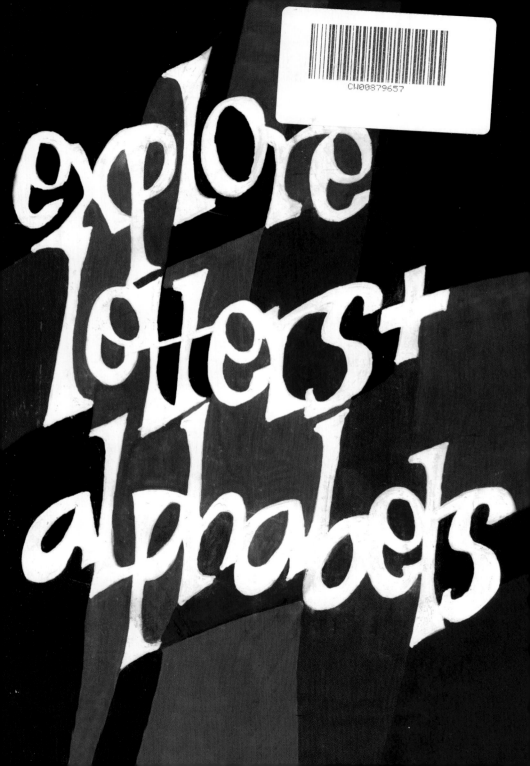

explore letters + alphabets

Published by

MELROSE BOOKS

An Imprint of Melrose Press Limited
St Thomas Place, Ely
Cambridgeshire
CB7 4GG, UK
www.melrosebooks.com

FIRST EDITION

Cover designed by Sava Savvas

ISBN 978 1 907040 38 2

Printed and bound in Malta by:
Latitude Press Ltd

The Task is Good and the Hope Great

For my children, Marina and Philip.

What is a palindrome?
It is a statement or word that reads identically backwards and forwards.

ACKNOWLEDGEMENTS

The writing of this book has relied upon the participation and encouragement of a number of people.

Thanks go to the students of the Red Maids School, Bristol and to Trinity School, Teignmouth, Devon for their contributions to some of the illustrations included.

To Mary Harley, whose love of lettering inspired a personal interest and wish to encourage everyone to see the pleasure to be derived from letter forms.

To Alan Mills for his support.

A special thanks to my children Marina and Philip and to my mother.

To Kathy Wagner-Kimbrough, for all her hard work and encouragement; Matt Stephens and to the rest of the team at Melrose Books, Ely.

The author tenders his grateful thanks to them all.

CONTENTS

SECTION TWO

SECTION THREE

INTRODUCTION

Explore Letters and Alphabets is a reference book with a practical function. It is a study of fourteen alphabets of the world in their historical context with practical exercises in which you, the reader, can get personally involved.

Letter forms and the different alphabets, including examples of how they have been used throughout the centuries, constitute the theme of the book.

Suggestions and calligraphic tasks will stimulate you to appreciate a wide range of styles, materials and techniques, encouraging a "hands on" involvement.

Letters are versatile forms and lend themselves to all manner of creative endeavour.

The main section of the book deals with the historical evolution, cultural variety and the possible relationship between alphabets. Actual location of these alphabets, in the form of accompanying illustrative material with practical examples, are included for clarification.

At the end of each alphabet section, you will find projects and practical work, i.e. ideas and suggestions, which will help you carry out your designs in your own art work.

In the second part of the book are the design values and visual appreciation exercises which, it is hoped, will focus your visual awareness of different letter forms.

A lot of the subject matter for the exercises is based on the practical work to be found in the main section of this book.

The third part of the book has the four questionnaires, with questions based on "Emotive", "Logos", "Letters in Action" and "Positive and Negative Relationships".

All the subject matter has been selected to show the wide range of styles, materials and techniques available.

"Like Rabbi Abulafia, I had learnt first of all the Hebrew alphabet. Like him, I loved to draw and to contemplate the big flowing letters; I was most at home with them and could make them long before I could do anything else with my hands.

It was such a pleasure to copy them from the prayer book, because in each letter there was some subtle part of the others, and as one learned to make the new ones, he discovered those familiar parts he already knew."

Ben Shahn.
Love and Joy about Letters.

USING ALPHABETS IN ART AND DESIGN

The aim of this book is to encourage awareness of some of the world's alphabets and their possible use in a creative and practical way.

It is written principally for reference, with practical exercises.

When you look at words you see letters which are the means of communicating with other people. Letters are everywhere. They glare at us in books, newspapers and magazines; they shout at us from traffic sign boards; and have a real impact on us when they scream their message from posters and advertisements.

How can we ignore them?

But letters are not just a means of communication. Whether using our own familiar alphabet or looking at other less familiar scripts, we are instantly aware of lines which are vertical, horizontal or diagonal; shapes made up of squares, triangles, circles or semi-circles; forms that are essentially architectural or organic; and the positive and negative spaces which exist between and around the letters.

Patterns and layouts of different styles of letters and their overall visual effect can make for interesting design.

Letters sharpen our visual awareness and encourage us to use them as a vehicle for personal expression.

The benefits of using this book are as follows:

- As a practical guide and useful reference in the use of different alphabets.
- It is of interest to a wide range of both adults and children.
- The possible use of letter forms can be utilised in other subject areas, not just in art.
- In a multi-cultural society, knowledge of different alphabets and the ways of communication they encourage can only help to foster understanding and a sense of harmony between different people and their cultures.
- The layout of the book, i.e. written text complementing illustrative material, makes a fairly complex subject much easier to assimilate.
- Using letters from different alphabets in our creative and design work helps us to "start off".

Ὅτι τὸ ζήτημα ᾧ ἐπιχειροῦμεν οὐ φαῦλον
ἀλλ' ὀξύ βλέποντος, ὡς ἐμοὶ φαίνεται. ἐπειδὴ
οὖν ἡμεῖς οὐ δεινοί, δοκῶ μοι, ἦν δ' ἐγώ, τοιαύτην
ποιήσασθαι ζήτησιν αὐτοῦ, οἷάνπερ ἂν εἰ
προσέταξέ τις γράμματα σμικρὰ πόρρωθεν
ἀναγνῶναι μὴ πάνυ ὀξὺ βλέπουσιν ἔπειτά
τις ἐνενόησεν, ὅτι τὰ αὐτὰ γράμματα
ἔστι που καὶ ἄλλοθι μείζω τέ καὶ ἐν
μείζονι, ἕρμαιον ἂν ἐφάνη οἶμαι ἐκεῖνα
πρῶτον ἀναγνόντας οὕτως ἐπισκοπεῖν τὰ
ἐλάττω, εἰ τὰ αὐτὰ ὄντα τυγχάνει.

ΠΛΑΤΩΝΟΣ – ΠΟΛΙΤΕΙΑΣ

"This is a very obscure subject we are enquiring into, and I think it needs very keen sight. We are not very clever, and so I think we had better proceed as follows. Let us suppose we are rather short-sighted men and are set to read a distant notice written in small letters. We then discover that the same notice is up elsewhere on a larger scale and in larger lettering. Won't it be a godsend to us to be able to read the larger notice first and then to compare it with the smaller to see if they are the same?

...When we were learning to read, we were not satisfied until we could recognise the letters of the alphabet wherever they occurred. We did not think them beneath our notice in large words or small, but tried to recognise them everywhere on the grounds that we should not have learned to read till we could.

That is true.

And we can't recognise reflections of the letters in water or in a mirror till we know the letters themselves.

The same process of learning gives us skill to recognise both."

Plato.
The Republic.

eXplore SECTION ONE

DESIGN VALUES AND LETTER FORMS

Can you imagine your life without letters?

Without an alphabet, how would you be able to communicate a quick written message to somebody, send a greetings card or letter to someone you love, take notes at a lecture?

You rely on letters and your personal ability to write correspondence and convey information using them. But letters are not just a means of communication. They have a design entity in themselves and because in each society and country they are familiar and easily recognisable they can be a basis to be used in different ways.

Every subject, whether it be a language, science or the arts, uses a specialist language and vocabulary appropriate to it to convey its meaning to others.

Art uses design values which are practical and these are line, colour, pattern, texture, and shape. Additional design values relevant to letter forms are contrast, edge, isolation, overlap, position, proportion, readability, rhythm, and space. These are explained on page 16 as is their use in artwork from the past and their interrelationship with other subjects.

When carrying out your practical work, you may need to use one or two or all five design values, as well as some of the additional ones. For example, Arabic-inspired letter types might be expressed using mostly lines; Illuminated and Celtic letters will make full use of colour, pattern and overlap; while Hebrew letters are very much based on shape and contrast. Chinese characters have strong pattern value and a clear isolation which makes one character distinct from another next to it. Conversely, certain design values lend themselves more readily to some alphabets than to others, so that proportion is inherent to Greek and Roman letters, while rhythm is very much evident in Armenian and Georgian.

By carrying out practical work using various media, and by expressing ideas using design values, your visual sensitivity and what you do in your artwork can be developed.

Another important addition to the above is to look at the ways letter forms have been incorporated in past art movements and by individual artists. For example, Hieroglyphics, with its individualistic pictorial imagery as wall surface decoration; Greek letters as adornment on buildings and pottery; Russian letters as an integral theme in icon painting; while the great Dutch artist, Rembrandt, often included letters in his masterpieces.

Other artists such as Juan Gris, Pablo Picasso, and George Braque made full use of letter forms in their analytical and synthetic Cubist work. Art movements in America in the 1950s and 1960s incorporated letter forms as seen in the work done by Roy Lichtenstein, Richard Hamilton and Andy Warhol.

Why not try carrying out work of your own based on all the alphabets in this book? Many examples are included to inspire you using a wide variety of media. Each of the alphabets by the very nature of their distinctive individuality has the power to inspire.

You learn about alphabets from doing.

Letters are a good way of "starting off".

DESIGN VALUES AND LETTER FORMS

DESIGN VALUES	AS RELEVANT TO LETTERS	AS HAVING A RELEVANCE TO OTHER MODES OF VISUAL COMMUNICATION
CONTRAST	an appreciation of balance and scale.	balance and scale can be put to use in personal hand-writing or in type layout.
EDGE	contours having either blurred or sharpley defined qualities.	a blurred edge makes an object look more distant.
ISOLATION	isolating a letter or word to stress importance.	the uniqueness of form meaning and emphasis.
OVERLAP	overlap letters to create scale and to attract and make impact. Depth.	the covering of one area by another. Strong surface decoration.
POSITION	Letters are part of their surroundings, yet by nature of their make up, positive/negative shapes; attention is abstract.	the relative placing of visual elements in a composition.
PROPORTION	as expressed in knowledge and skills related to perceptual analytical and critical faculties.	measurement of the human body - in the distance between the rows of branches of a young fir tree.
RHYTHM	flowing movement in letters: aesthetic layout of type on page.	comparison with waves on water. tonal effects in a composition or fabric material.
READABILITY	Letters have to be discerned quickly; they must make an impression and leave direct impact	human capacity for spatial judgement; human eye can then structure what it sees.
SPACE	comparative differences in positive/negative letter areas.	arrangements of space can alter drastically from letter to letter and from picture to picture.

MODES	ART APPRECIATION AND HISTORY	INTERRELATION WITH OTHER SUBJECTS	DESIGN ELEMENTS
handwriting typing books	Op Art Hebrew alphabet gothic letters.	needlework, woodwork home economics map reading natural flags.	SHAPE
composition fabric printing lino cutting	Egyptian hieroglyphics architecture	Geometry Woodwork. clay tiles	
headings posters	Chinese and Japanese characters.	geometry. drama	TEXTURE
montage wallpaper design fabric printing	illuminated letters Celtic alphabet Art Nouveau.	Needlework building perspective.	
montage wallpaper design fabric printing graphic forms composition	Islamic painting and architecture Hieroglyphics Russian letters. Gothic letters.	Geography, Geometry woodwork, map-reading. book covers.	PATTERN
life drawing perspective design	greek and Roman alphabet Renaissance frescoes Classical buildings illuminated letters	Mathematics building. furniture sculpture.	
fabric printing life drawing painting	Arabic Georgian } letters Armenian Celtic letters.	Movement and dance. Drama, Physical Education	COLOUR
improvement of handwriting	Roman letter on Trajan column and public buildings. Toulouse-Lautrec posters-road signs.	general reading typing.	
silhouette	Pop Art Op Art Chinese and Japanese alphabets.	geography building.	LINE

17

HISTORICAL DEVELOPMENT

Letters are the means by which mankind records words and ideas. As they are an essential part of everyday life, thought and action are directed through them in the form of writing, signs, books, documents, posters, graphics, and aesthetic logos.

Through the ages, letters have evolved and changed as the development of mankind has progressed.

The alphabet began as pictures in Egypt and Mesopotamia and, indeed, all writing seems to have started as pictures. Pictures became the accepted way in early times as the need to record the spoken word allowed people to understand and communicate.

In the beginning, written records were drawn with fingers dipped in wild plant juice or animal blood. Over periods of time, the pictures were established into a convention both in meaning and form so that thoughts and ideas were not misunderstood. What was originally a picture became a sign representing an idea as well as a thing.

The letter X is an early example of a made sign. Traders pointed to the goods to be traded and then crossed their fingers. So crossed fingers symbolised an exchange. This sign appears frequently in ancient scripts in mankind's early history.

Roughly 3500 B.C., the Cuneiform alphabet evolved. The Sumerians cut the end of a reed to a triangular shape and pressed little wedge-shaped marks on wet clay tablets which were baked in the sun. This alphabet, created in Mesopotamia between the two great rivers of the Tigris and Euphrates, had approximately 600 symbols to convey and record information.

From this time, man has lived in a civilisation of the recorded word of letters.

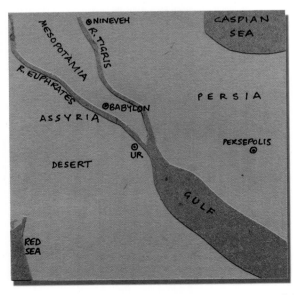

Different systems of writing developed in different parts of the world.

The Egyptians made a writing material from the pith of the papyrus plant which grew in the marshlands of the Nile. This made a hard, tough paper which lasted for thousands of years – the word paper is derived from papyrus. On it they wrote with stiff little brushes made by fraying the ends of thin reeds. Because the brush gave curved lines, writing on papyrus caused the writing to change from the original carved Hieroglyphic reserved for important buildings into a form known as Hieratic (Greek – sacred).

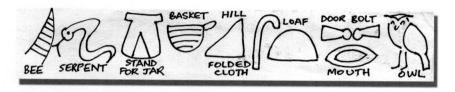

In China the picture characters were painted with a soft brush on silk or paper and the lines tended to follow the strokes of the brush. It is from China that paper was introduced to the western world by Arab merchants in the twelfth century. They are credited also with the invention of printing although this "mechanised form of communication" was developed by Gutenberg in Germany in the fifteenth century.

The Chinese alphabet of roughly 250,000 ideograms (a sign standing for an idea and not a sound) is today used by over one billion people.

Western civilisation has frequently traced two routes: the Hebrew for religion and the Greek for art, architecture, politics, drama, literature, and science. The essential thread linking and stimulating both has been the alphabet. In the past, it was the custom to refer to an alphabet by the names of the first two or three letters. The origin of the word ALPHABET is clearly recognisable in the first two letters of the Greek alphabet, ΑΛΦΑ ΒΗΤΑ; in Hebrew, aleph – beth.

The Armenian alphabet has been influenced in its formation by Greek letters.

When the Romans conquered Greece, they took over the Greek alphabet but changed the shape of some letters. They used square letters on stone and rounded letters for writing. It is the most widely used alphabet in the world today.

The Cyrillic (Russian) alphabet, which is one of the youngest of the world's alphabets, is approximately 1000 years old and resembles Greek.

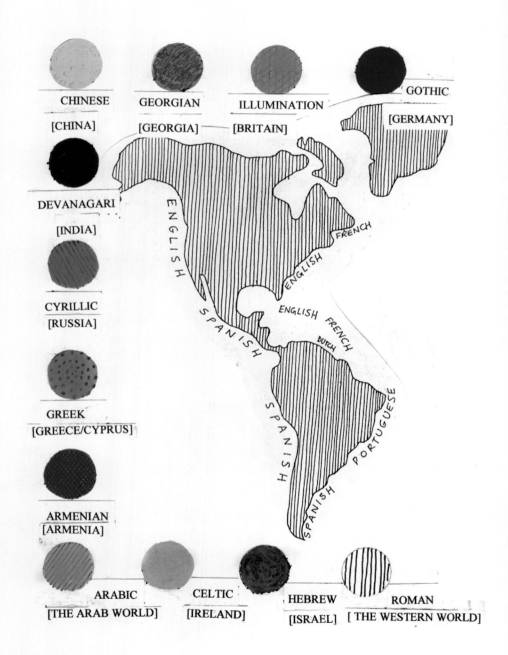

CHINESE
[CHINA]

GEORGIAN
[GEORGIA]

ILLUMINATION
[BRITAIN]

GOTHIC
[GERMANY]

DEVANAGARI
[INDIA]

CYRILLIC
[RUSSIA]

GREEK
[GREECE/CYPRUS]

ARMENIAN
[ARMENIA]

ARABIC
[THE ARAB WORLD]

CELTIC
[IRELAND]

HEBREW
[ISRAEL]

ROMAN
[THE WESTERN WORLD]

ENGLISH

FRENCH

ENGLISH

ENGLISH FRENCH

DUTCH

SPANISH

SPANISH

PORTUGUESE

SPANISH

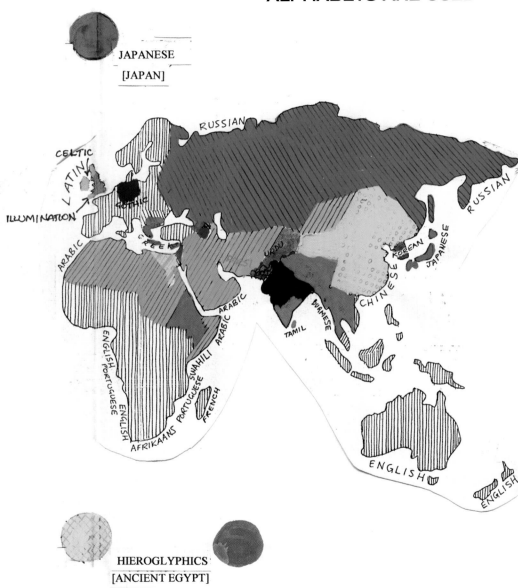

JAPANESE
[JAPAN]

HIEROGLYPHICS
[ANCIENT EGYPT]

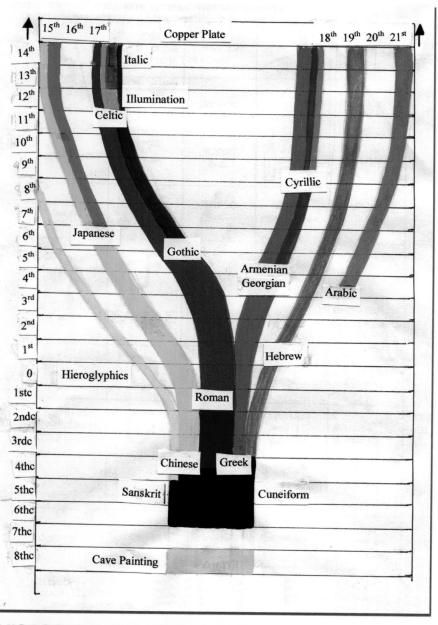

HISTORICAL DEVELOPMENT OF ALPHABETS

24

"If you have a long external wall, paint the school name in huge letters thereon. If you have a low-storied building, spell out the letters of the school title along the classroom windows. If you are in a tall, many-floored school, hang the letters vertically downwards.

Don't skulk behind the walls; emblazon the school and its name and its motif as much as possible."

E. Midwinter.
Education for Sale.

THE 14 ALPHABETS

The fourteen alphabets covered in this book appear according to their estimated chronological development. Please refer to the previous pages of "Historical Development" and "Where Some of the World's Alphabets are Used".

HIEROGLYPHICS (sacred signs) – created circa 4000 B.C. are the characters used in the writing system of ancient Egypt, in which pictures of people and things were used to represent words or sounds.

The direction of writing is normally from right to left, the sign facing the beginning of the line.

The ancient Egyptians called their written texts "the words of the Gods".

Down through the centuries the script retained a sacred character and more or less magical powers. Anybody who knew how to write the approximately seven hundred signs which constituted Egyptian "letters", each sign representing a sound or an object, was held in great esteem.

In its early development, reed, chisel, and pen were used on papyrus and buildings.

CHINESE – 250,000 characters – pictograms (stylised pictures) – created roughly 3500 B.C. In its early development, brushes and ink on silk, paper and pottery.

The Chinese language is very old, so old in fact that inscriptions that are possibly 8,000 years old have been uncovered, and these early letters are probably the forerunners of Chinese characters. Chinese script in use 3,500 years ago is still in use today.

The earliest characters were pictograms i.e. stylised pictures of objects and phenomena such as animals, sun, moon, and man.

There is also a secondary category of characters which are ideographs e.g. – means one, is two, is three.

Characters are thus formed by combining pictograms with ideographs.

Chinese is spoken by more people than any other language in the world. A dictionary will contain as many as 50,000 words.

Chinese children learn about 2,000 characters by the time they are in secondary school. To read a newspaper you must know two or three times that number of words. To depict a single character/letter you may need to use as many as 33 strokes.

THE DEVANAGARI ALPHABET (Sanskrit – "letters hanging from a line") – 48 letters – 3500 B.C. In its early development, pen and ink in manuscripts using brush and paint.

One of the main languages of India is written in an alphabet called Devanagari, often referred to simply as Nagari. This alphabet is mostly used in the north and central states of the country.

Hindi, the main language of India, and Urdu, the language of Pakistan, are sometimes referred to as Hindustani. Hindi and Urdu are sister languages and share the same grammar, and many words are the same. But while Hindi is written in Devanagari, Urdu is written in a script devised from both Arabic and Persian.

Although both languages are written with different scripts, they belong to the "extended family" which has a common ancestor in Sanskrit, the classical Indian language.

Devanagari roughly means "Scripts of the City of the Gods". It runs from left to right. There is no distinction between capital and lower case letters.

Handwriting follows the printed forms. The basic unit of this alphabet is the syllable and not so much the individual letter as in the Roman alphabet.

HEBREW ("square letters of symmetry") – 22 letters – 3000 B.C. In its early development, pen and ink on scrolls were used.

Hebrew distinguishes between two alphabets, early Hebrew prior to the sixth century B.C., and the classical or square. It is one of the world's oldest languages and is written and spoken today in much the same way as it was more than 2,000 years ago. The early Hebrew alphabet, like the modern script, had 22 letters and both scripts are written from right to left on a straight line.

The Dead Sea Scrolls

When Jesus lived in the Holy Land, there were several Jewish sects. One of these sects called themselves the Essenes and it is these people who may have written the Dead Sea Scrolls.

In this collection of documents, the earliest surviving books of the Bible are included. In addition, there are also sectarian writings and sacred Hebrew canon.

GREEK ("architectural, organic, and angular letters") – 24 letters – 3000 B.C. In its early development, the stylus, chisel and brush were used on pottery, statues, graves and buildings.

It was the Greeks who made the momentous decision to write from left to right, starting each time from the left margin, some time in the sixth century. Until then, their written matter had been "boustrophedon" ("as the ox plough"), a technical term for alternate direction writing – the way a farmer ploughs his field.

Greek letters in ancient times were to be found painted principally on clay pots where they were very much part of the overall design of the vessel, or they appear carved into the marble surface of a temple or tombstone called "stele", where they commemorate the dead person. Some priceless manuscripts written in Greek are to be found in the monasteries on holy Mount Athos in northern Greece, and St Catherine's Monastery in Sinai, Egypt.

"The Greeks had a word for it" – this proverb is a reminder of the richness of Greek vocabulary.

Greek is the first language of western civilisation and is considered by many to be the most effective and admirable means of communication ever devised. The following prefixes and suffixes taken from Greek are to be found in the English language:

Poly = much/many	Micro = small
Anti = against	Hetero = different
Auto = self	Hem = half
Geo = earth	Hydro = water
Litho = stone	Tele = distance
Physio = nature	Psych = mind
Photo = light	Phono = sound
Mega = large	Philo = love
Meter = measure	Scope = see
Gram = letter	Graph = write
Phobia = fear	

THE ROMAN ALPHABET ("letters of harmony and proportion") – 26 letters – 1500 B.C. In its early development, stylus and chisel on papyrus, wax tablet, triumphal arches and public buildings.

The Romans were greatly influenced by the Greeks but they had three main ways of using their letter forms:

1. They carved inscriptions in stone, e.g. triumphal arches as well as on temples.

2. They used rolls of papyrus for books.

3. Notes and messages were inscribed on wooden tablets which were covered in wax. An instrument called a "stylus" was used to scratch into the wax. The stylus had a pointed end while the other, rounded end was used for rubbing out mistakes.

Roman letters are made up of horizontal, vertical, and diagonal lines as well as curves, circles, and semi-circles.

After the conquest of Greece in the first century B.C., Y and Z were adopted and placed at the end of the alphabet.

The "new" Latin alphabet contained 23 letters. In the Middle Ages, J was added and U and W also, so as to distinguish them from V.

So J, U, W, Y and Z were not originally part of the Roman alphabet.

ARABIC ("flowing lines of beauty") – 28 letters – fourth century. In its early development, the chisel, pen, and brush on scrolls, tiles, walls and buildings were used.

Arabic letters have played a particularly important role in Islamic art. Not only has it been venerated as the main means of artistic expression, it is used because Islam does not allow visual depiction of the human image in such a place of worship as a mosque.

Arabic script is usually painted on exquisite tiles which cover the walls of mosques and important buildings. Poetry was also highly venerated, and expressed through calligraphy as well as floral motifs and geometrical designs.

Arabic letters are basically consonants, so vowel signs are indicated by marks which appear above or below the letter. Arabic, the language of the Koran, has remained largely unchanged since the seventh century and the script/letters have been employed by other languages, namely Persian, Urdu, and Pashto.

ARMENIAN ("walking sticks") – 39 letters. In its early development, pen and ink in manuscripts.

The Armenian alphabet was created in 406 A.D. by Mesrop Mastoc and consists of 39 letters. When he created the alphabet, he was guided by the principle that each letter should represent only one sound. Until Mesrop's time, the Armenians used the Greek alphabet for all their written correspondence.

Armenian writing proceeds from left to right. The first sentence to be written in the alphabet stated "recognise wisdom and advice, heed the word of the genius".

Armenian letters are vertical with flowing curves and indeed look like walking sticks.

GEORGIAN ("the alphabet with no capital letters") – 33 letters – fifth century A.D. In its early development, pen and ink in books and manuscripts.

Written Georgian goes back to the fifth century and it is a language with a rich literature. It is derived in its basic system from the Greek alphabet. Remarkably, the Georgian alphabet has no capital letters so proper nouns are not capitalised in that language. The oldest known manuscript written in Georgian (864 A.D) is to be found in St Catherine's Monastery in Sinai, Egypt.

A characteristic of the language is the liberal use of consonants that are present in amazing variety.

Georgians call themselves Kartvelebi and call their country Sakartvelo.

CELTIC ("letters of intricate pattern") – originally 18 letters – fifth century A.D. In its early development, pen, ink, brush and paint were used in books, manuscripts, and on tombstones.

"Celts" comes from the Latin Celtae, to describe people who lived in the northern fringes of their world. Herodotus (484–424 B.C.) tells of Celtic settlements near the source of the Danube.

Celtic tradition survived most strongly in the outer fringes of Europe and especially Ireland. Celtic art took on a new lease of life in manuscript illumination. Ireland has produced some of the greatest works such as the "Book of Kells", which dates from about 800 A.D.

The Celts decorated practical objects with intricate patterns to be found on high crosses covered with biblical carvings, weapons, armour, cups, and books.

The traditional Celtic/Gaelic alphabet evolved from the Roman one and contained five vowels and thirteen consonants; J, K, Q, V, W, X, Y and Z were missing. There are many more sounds so the Celtic languages combine letters to convey sounds not covered by single letters.

JAPANESE ("pictograms") – 46 letters – fifth century A.D. In its early development, pen, brush and ink were used in books, on hangings and on pottery.

There are four scripts in Japanese: Kanji, Hiragana, Katakana and Romaji. Each has its own special function.

Kanji, originally from China, has today an approved number of 1,945 characters for daily use. These are needed to read a newspaper properly.

Hiragana means rounded, easy-to-use characters, both in the shape and relative simplicity of the script. The Hiragana symbols were developed by simplifying Kanji.

Katakana means partial, because the characters were developed from Kanji, but they are more angular in shape, while Hiragana are more rounded.

Romaji are the western alphabet.

Kanji ☼ → ϴ → ☉ → 日 SUN

Hiranga あいうえお a i u e o

Katakana アイウエオ a i u e o

CYRILLIC ("variation on a theme") – 33 letters – ninth century A.D. In its early development, pen, brush and paint on icons, churches, and posters.

The Russian alphabet, which is one of the youngest of the world's alphabets, resembles the Greek. In the ninth century, a Greek monk called Cyril devised the Cyrillic – Russian – alphabet. It was based on Greek letters with some Latin letters as well, and some additional letters which correspond to distinctive Russian sounds.

Until the end of the eighteenth century, the written alphabet of Russia was Old Church Slavonic. This alphabet formed the basis of Ukrainian and Belarussian also. The old style alphabet was simplified in 1918 by the Bolsheviks.

The Russian alphabet is made up of consonants and vowels plus a couple of letters which have no sound of their own, but which affect the sound of other letters. The handwritten alphabet is only a little different from the printed version in books.

Russian letters form an integral part of a Russian icon, as they do all Orthodox icons. The letters are usually painted on wood using gold leaf, and are dedicated to a particular saint, or depict a momentous event in the New Testament such as The Annunciation, Crucifixion etc.

SPECIAL ALPHABETS. Gothic, Illumination and Italic are not strictly distinct alphabets in their own right as they use Roman letters. However, from a design point of view, they are worthy of study and are included in this book.

GOTHIC, or Blackletter, evolved in the early part of the thirteenth century and was used in northern Europe, particularly Germany, until the early sixteenth century.

Initially, parchment was in short supply, which necessitated more letters being written on a page. Because the heavy black letters were closely spaced, the completed pages just looked black. Johannes Gutenberg printed his first book around 1450 in this style of letter. In fact, his book was the first to be printed with movable type. He is generally considered the inventor of printing using separate pieces of metal for each letter.

ILLUMINATION/ILLUSTRATION. In the Middle Ages the letters used in writing for the beautiful illuminated manuscripts were very much in the hands of the Church. Monks used to inscribe and decorate the Gospels by hand with elaborate, highly-coloured letters. In addition to the monks, some priests were used as "civil" servants, whose job it was to write out official and legal records rather than artistic works.

ITALIC. The Roman alphabet has changed and developed with extraordinary adaptability over the centuries. It was in Renaissance Italy in the fifteenth century that scribes rediscovered the classical inscriptions in manuscripts, and a reaction set in against the Gothic style. Until then, books had been very scarce and few people were educated enough to read them or able to afford to buy them. As people became more prosperous and books became available to a wider group of people, the need to write and paint encouraged a quicker method of recording material. The Italic style of letter evolved, where letters were "joined up", slanting slightly forward so as to be written quickly using a quill pen.

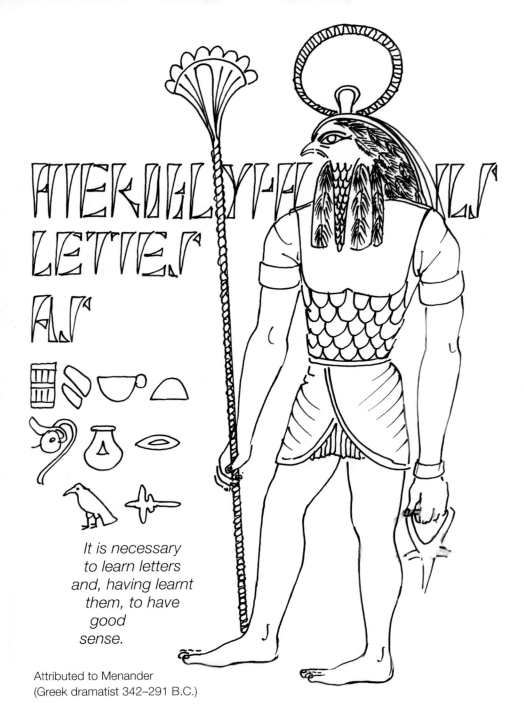

HIEROGLYPHICS
LETTER
A S

*It is necessary
to learn letters
and, having learnt
them, to have
good
sense.*

Attributed to Menander
(Greek dramatist 342–291 B.C.)

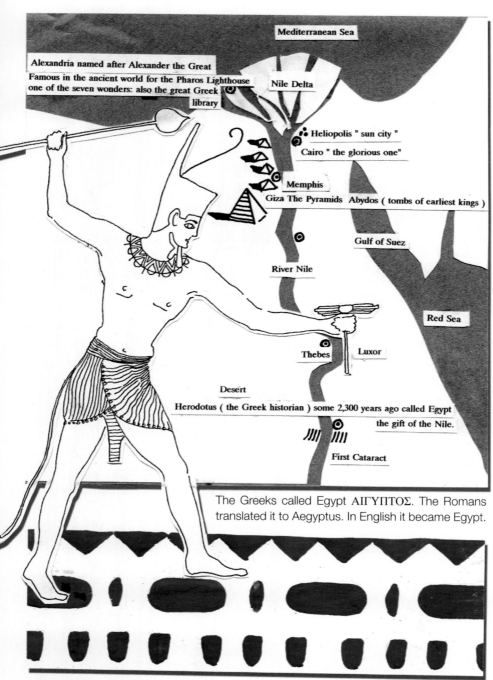

Mediterranean Sea

Alexandria named after Alexander the Great
Famous in the ancient world for the Pharos Lighthouse
one of the seven wonders: also the great Greek
library

Nile Delta

Heliopolis " sun city "

Cairo " the glorious one"

Memphis
Giza The Pyramids Abydos (tombs of earliest kings)

Gulf of Suez

River Nile

Red Sea

Thebes   Luxor

Desert

Herodotus (the Greek historian) some 2,300 years ago called Egypt
the gift of the Nile.

First Cataract

The Greeks called Egypt ΑΙΓΥΠΤΟΣ. The Romans
translated it to Aegyptus. In English it became Egypt.

Wall decoration 1500 B.C.

HIEROGLYPHIC ALPHABET

HIEROGLYPHICS

Hieroglyphics means sacred writing or sacred carving. It evolved into a stylised picture "alphabet" roughly 3,000 years ago. The letter types were 24 signs in number, and they stood for objects, pictograms, ideas, ideograms and sounds. These letter types were usually written from right to left, but sometimes vertically as well.

The Egyptians cut pictures on stone or clay, or wrote on papyrus with black or red ink (i.e. soot or ochre mixed with gum). Little brushes were used for drawing pictures.

Literacy was greatly valued in ancient Egypt. Scribes recorded important events and the great variety of signs had to be learnt by heart and in the right order. This was usually the job of well-trained slaves.

Egypt was later frequently ruled by Greeks, e.g. Ptolemy, Cleopatra. The court language was Greek, especially in Alexandria which became a great centre of learning. The original 24-letter Egyptian alphabet had a great influence on other alphabets (Greek has 24 letters).

The 24-letter Hieroglyphic alphabet. Skill and scholarship were needed to master the written language. Scribes were often educated slaves.

The Egyptians cut pictures on stone or clay or wrote on papyrus with black or red ink, using a reed with a frayed end that made a stiff brush.

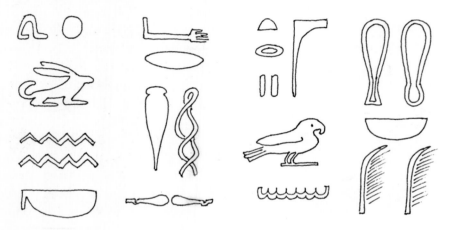

This is the name of an official, written in Hieroglyphics.

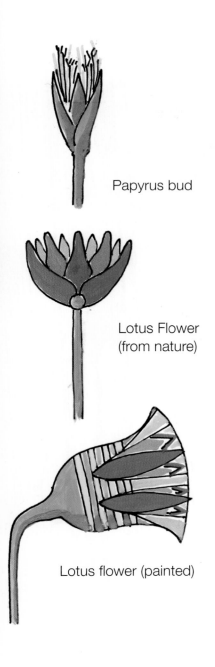

Papyrus bud

Lotus Flower (from nature)

Lotus flower (painted)

To make papyrus, remove the green coat of the rush and cut the stem into strips.

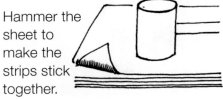

Hammer the sheet to make the strips stick together.

Roll the sheet which will then make a thin, smooth paper ready for use.

OLD

These two examples using the word "old" are figurative pictograms based on appropriate letter shapes. The figurative pictograms were inspired by paintings of people on Egyptian buildings.

In Egyptian art, people are always shown in a stylised combination of face, legs and feet, sideways or in a profile; while the body or torso is shown front view. These positions are without perspective, as solid form was not introduced until the Renaissance period in Italy.

Pictograms are an essential part of modern society as they transmit their message instantly to the observer. They are particularly effective when designed as simply as possible, and executed in bright colours which enhance the message and attract the eye.

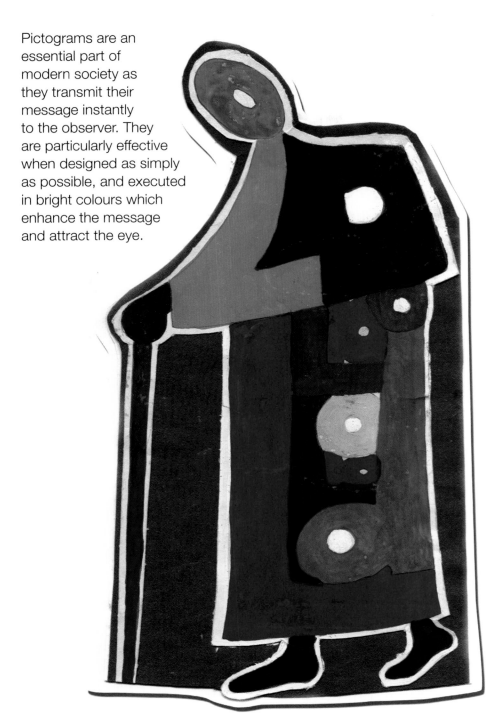

PROJECTS – PRACTICAL WORK

Ideas and suggestions for practical work

How Hieroglyphics characters can be used by you:

- SYMBOLS are very much part of communication today. Hieroglyphic-type messages and symbols can be designed and used in SCHOOL showing directions to different departments; around the OFFICE giving instructions; and decorating a WALL for exhibition displays.

Materials

Pencils, felt-tips, poster paint and brushes, pen and ink. The examples shown will give you ideas as to what you can do.

Pictograms in use today – simplified figurative shapes to denote public conveniences.

Tired.
The word is enacting its meaning using pictogram-type letters.

Pictogram letters based on the bird as a subject.

LETTER PLAY – HAVING FUN WITH VISUALS

Two ways of looking at ideograms

Now that you have a good idea what can be done with pictograms, look at the symbols below and:

- Write the appropriate message conveyed to the symbols in column (a).
- Write the appropriate letter from D, E, A, O, M in column (b).
- Consider what other ideas you can think of.

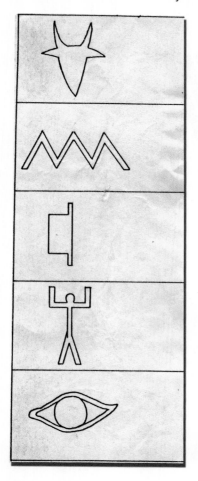
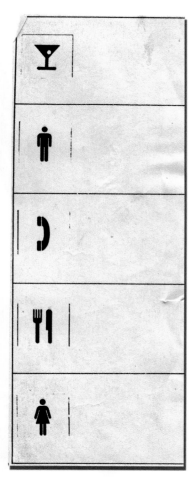

These ideograms stand for "China". This is what the Chinese people call their country – "Middle Kingdom".

中 Middle

國 kingdom

人 people

壽 long life

45

THE CHINESE ALPHABET

Chinese, which is the oldest living script, is made up of ideograms: characters symbolizing ideas of things.

The origins of the Chinese alphabet can be said to go back as far as 5000 B.C. The Chinese characters in use today are the descendants of the script of the Shang Period. There are around 250,000 written characters of which roughly 5000 characters are commonly used on a daily basis. Ninety per cent of China's population use the written language of Han, the largest ethnic group.

Chinese is a system of ideographs which are based on pictures. Every idea has a picture that expresses it. The first character for "China" is a box with a vertical line running through it, meaning "central" and is the first character of Middle Kingdom, as the Chinese call their country.

As the Chinese writing system is open-ended, letters are continuously being added to the "alphabet". Words are constantly being added and letters must be invented when new symbols are needed.

The average Chinese person recognises around 2–3,000 forms, the basic literacy necessary to read newspapers and magazines. A scholar might know 10,000 ideographs.

Calligraphy means "beautiful writing" and is considered by the Chinese, along with painting, to be the ultimate art form, and has a special place in their culture. Brush and ink, stick and paper or silk are used in both painting and calligraphy. A painting can be enhanced by calligraphy and it becomes an integral part of it.

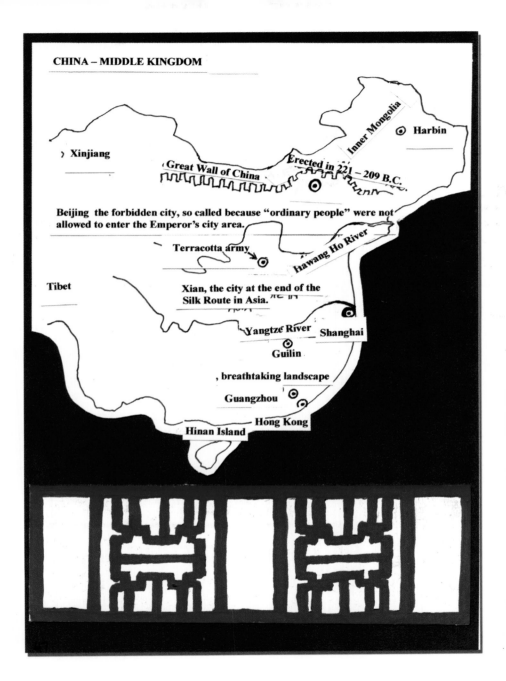

CHINA – MIDDLE KINGDOM

Xinjiang

Inner Mongolia

Harbin

Great Wall of China

Erected in 221 – 209 B.C.

Beijing the forbidden city, so called because "ordinary people" were not allowed to enter the Emperor's city area.

Terracotta army

Hawang Ho River

Tibet

Xian, the city at the end of the Silk Route in Asia.

Yangtze River

Shanghai

Guilin

, breathtaking landscape

Guangzhou

Hong Kong

Hinan Island

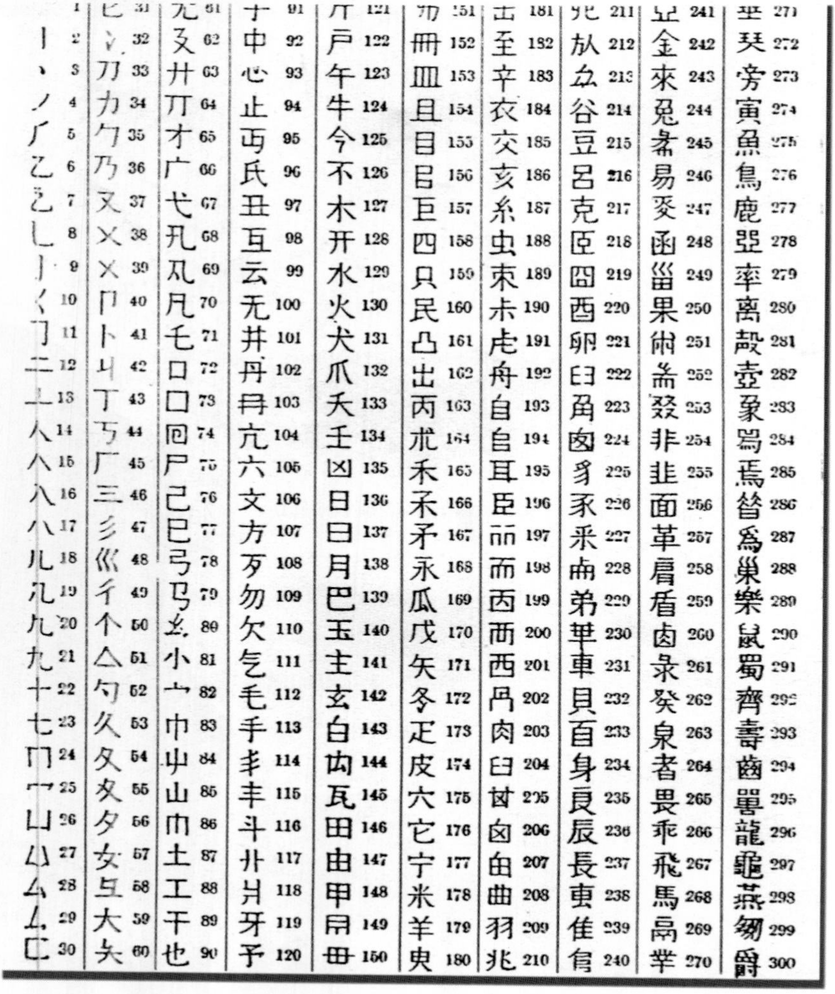

一 1	匕 31	尢 61	于 91	斤 121	[illegible] 151	古 181	兆 211	[illegible] 241	[illegible] 271
丨 2	冫 32	及 62	中 92	戶 122	冊 152	至 182	㫃 212	金 242	巽 272
丶 3	刀 33	廾 63	心 93	午 123	皿 153	辛 183	㐺 213	來 243	旁 273
丿 4	力 34	丌 64	止 94	牛 124	且 154	衣 184	谷 214	兔 244	寅 274
𠂆 5	勹 35	才 65	丏 95	今 125	目 155	交 185	豆 215	彖 245	魚 275
乙 6	乃 36	广 66	氏 96	不 126	㠯 156	亥 186	呂 216	易 246	鳥 276
乙 7	又 37	弋 67	丑 97	木 127	巨 157	糸 187	克 217	受 247	鹿 277
乚 8	乂 38	孔 68	互 98	开 128	四 158	虫 188	臣 218	函 248	[illegible] 278
亅 9	㐅 39	卂 69	云 99	水 129	只 159	束 189	囧 219	甾 249	率 279
𡿨 10	冂 40	凡 70	无 100	火 130	民 160	朿 190	酉 220	果 250	离 280
𠃍 11	卜 41	乇 71	井 101	犬 131	凸 161	虍 191	卵 221	[illegible] 251	殸 281
二 12	丩 42	口 72	丹 102	爪 132	出 162	舟 192	臼 222	希 252	壺 282
亠 13	丁 43	囗 73	冄 103	夭 133	丙 163	自 193	角 223	癹 253	象 283
人 14	丂 44	冋 74	亢 104	壬 134	朮 164	自 194	肉 224	非 254	舄 284
入 15	厂 45	尸 75	六 105	凶 135	禾 165	耳 195	豸 225	韭 255	焉 285
八 16	三 46	己 76	文 106	日 136	禾 166	臣 196	豕 226	面 256	晉 286
八 17	彡 47	巳 77	方 107	曰 137	矛 167	而 197	釆 227	革 257	爲 287
儿 18	巛 48	弓 78	歹 108	月 138	永 168	而 198	甫 228	眉 258	巢 288
几 19	彳 49	马 79	勿 109	巴 139	瓜 169	西 199	弟 229	盾 259	樂 289
九 20	个 50	幺 80	欠 110	玉 140	戊 170	西 200	[illegible] 230	卣 260	鼠 290
九 21	亼 51	小 81	气 111	主 141	矢 171	西 201	車 231	彔 261	蜀 291
十 22	勺 52	⺍ 82	毛 112	玄 142	冬 172	冎 202	貝 232	癸 262	齊 292
七 23	久 53	巾 83	手 113	白 143	疋 173	肉 203	百 233	泉 263	壽 293
冂 24	夂 54	屮 84	丯 114	[illegible] 144	皮 174	臼 204	身 234	者 264	齒 294
冖 25	夊 55	山 85	丰 115	瓦 145	穴 175	甘 205	艮 235	畏 265	[illegible] 295
凵 26	夕 56	巿 86	斗 116	田 146	它 176	囟 206	辰 236	乖 266	龍 296
凵 27	女 57	土 87	卝 117	由 147	宁 177	甶 207	長 237	飛 267	龜 297
厶 28	彑 58	工 88	爿 118	甲 148	米 178	曲 208	叀 238	馬 268	燕 298
厶 29	大 59	干 89	牙 119	用 149	羊 179	羽 209	隹 239	高 269	[illegible] 299
匚 30	夨 60	也 90	予 120	毌 150	臾 180	兆 210	[illegible] 240	丵 270	爵 300

CHINESE CHARACTERS (letters)

By tradition, Chinese characters can be divided into six different types according to how many strokes are used to write them. The easiest characters are usually made up of two strokes and are most often used for familiar words. Look at the list of Chinese characters from 1–300. The characters get increasingly complex further down the list. The individual strokes can be used singly or combined so as to change their meaning.

The Chinese wrote on paper or silk, with a soft thickish brush and black ink. The ink was made in blocks and ground with water into a sort of paint.

The Chinese writer uses his brush to express himself aesthetically while remaining clearly legible. Brushes are usually goat hair inserted into bamboo handles.

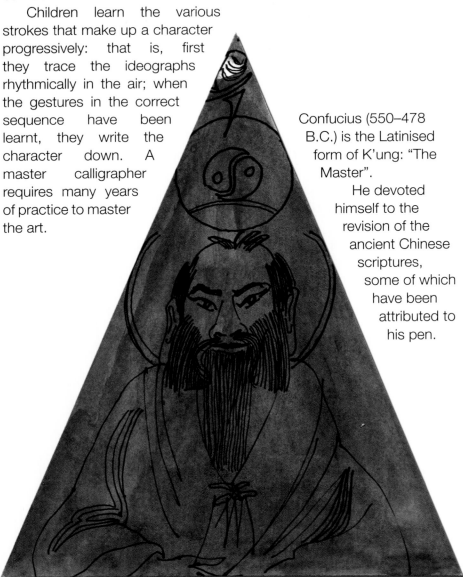

Children learn the various strokes that make up a character progressively: that is, first they trace the ideographs rhythmically in the air; when the gestures in the correct sequence have been learnt, they write the character down. A master calligrapher requires many years of practice to master the art.

Confucius (550–478 B.C.) is the Latinised form of K'ung: "The Master".

He devoted himself to the revision of the ancient Chinese scriptures, some of which have been attributed to his pen.

China is a land of many languages. The Chinese language itself is as diverse as the country and there are many dialects, as one would expect for the third largest country, in area, on earth. The Cantonese speaker in the south cannot speak to the northerner talking in Mandarin.

Putonghua literally means "ordinary languages", and is taught in every school. This is based on the language of Beijing and the north. Other languages in China, and there are many, include Tibetan, Mongol, Manchu, Zhuang, Uygur, Yi, Miao, and Dong.

English words of Chinese origin are: tea, typhoon, kaolin, and kumquat.

Confucianism means social order and responsibility, respect for parents, elders and authorities, and veneration for the ancestors.

Yin and Yang is the union of the negative and positive principles.

Chinese letters are based on drawings representing either concrete objects or symbols. It is an ideographic language with a different sign for each idea or object.

Beautiful calligraphy that reveals a rich personality is valued as highly as any scholastic achievement.

Block printing of letters was a Chinese invention (like fireworks).

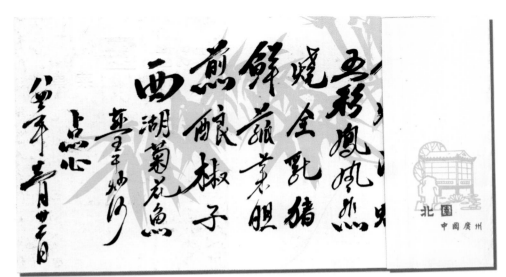

Some examples of entry tickets of various types, menus etc in China today incorporating Chinese and Roman alphabet letters.

THE GREAT WALL 长城

HERITAGE SITE OF CULTURAL ANTHROPOLOGY

Tickets and menus.

TWELVE ANIMALS OF THE CHINESE ZODIAC

鼠牛虎兔龍蛇馬羊猴雞狗豬

RAT			OX			TIGER		
	1936	1972		1937	1973		1938	1974
	1948	1984		1949	1985		1950	1986
	1960	1996		1961	1997		1962	1998
RABBIT			DRAGON			SNAKE		
	1939	1975		1940	1976		1941	1977
	1951	1987		1952	1988		1953	1989
	1963	1999		1964	2000		1965	2001
HORSE			GOAT			MONKEY		
	1942	1978		1943	1979		1944	1980
	1954	1990		1955	1991		1956	1992
	1966	2002		1967	2003		1968	2004
ROOSTER			DOG			PIG		
	1945	1981		1946	1982		1947	1983
	1957	1993		1958	1994		1959	1995
	1969	2005		1970	2006		1971	2007

雁塔吉祥生肖增驛祿

Individual animal signs of the Da Cien Temple
are bound to bring you blessings and benefits

CHINA XI

大雁塔 DA YAN PAGODA

place for stamping

京菜

Peking Food
Recommended Menus

Barbecued Peking Duck
北京填鴨

Beggar's Chicken Dish
敦化雞

Sautéed Beef with Spring Onion Served on
Sizzling Platter
鐵板蔥爆牛柳絲

Pan-Fried King Prawns in Brown Sauce
乾燒明蝦

Shark's Fin, Heart of Cabbage, Chicken
Double Boiled in Clay Pot
砂鍋菜胆雞燉翅

Mo Su Pork
木須肉

Cooking

Chinese cooking is greatly appreciated all over the world. Here are some
well-known examples in both Chinese and English.

Cold Cuts Combination
燒味拼盤

Shark's Fin Soup with Shredded Chicken
紅燒雞絲翅

Poached Shrimps
白灼蝦

Sweet & Sour Pork
生炒排骨/咕嚕肉

Deep Fried Duckling with Mashed Taro
荔茸香酥鴨

Roast Pigeon
燒乳鴿

How both Chinese and Roman alphabet letters can be used to complement each other for a menu.

Hong Kong - London

香港 · 倫敦

Lunch
Mesclun salad with shrimp
sesame soy dressing

午餐
明蝦拼鮮蔬沙律
配芝蔴豉油汁

Braised spring chicken with preserved turnip
steamed rice and broccoli
or
Pan-fried fish fillet with pesto and tomato sauce
boiled potatoes, green beans
and roasted pumpkin with herbs
or
Penne rigate with spinach, nutmeg and
Parmesan sauce

燒春雞
配白飯及西蘭花
或
香草蕃茄汁魚柳
配馬鈴薯、四季豆及香草南瓜
或
芝士汁菠菜豆蔻意式通心粉

Chocolate layer cake

朱古力蛋糕

Tea and coffee

茶及咖啡

Dinner
Mixed seasonal fruit

晚餐
時令雜果

Sauteed fish fillet with sa cha sauce
steamed rice,
Chinese long cabbage with fried bean curd
or
Braised lamb stew
mash potato with mustard pommery,
green beans with onion julienne and
roasted pumpkin

沙茶醬魚柳
配白飯及豆乾津白
或
燴羊肉
配芥末薯蓉、洋葱青豆及南瓜

Caramelized vanilla bean panna cotta

呍呢拿椰子蛋糕

Tea and coffee

茶及咖啡

Snack
Snacks are available throughout the flight.

小食
航機上另備有小食供閣下隨時享用。

A number of factors distinguish Chinese painting from the west and these include composition, subject, and materials, through to attitude, purpose, and appreciation.

PROJECTS – PRACTICAL WORK

tree

Ideas and suggestions for practical work

How Chinese characters can be used by you:

- Try printing some Chinese characters. You will need good quality brushes of different thicknesses, and black/Indian drawing ink and fine cartridge paper.
- A wall-hanging – letters with flowers and perhaps birds.
- A brochure – to publicise an oriental garden.
- A menu – for a Chinese meal.

2 trees/ grove

Materials:

Pencils for sketching initial ideas, brushes and inks and black ink, poster paints.
The examples shown will give you ideas as to what you can do.

3 trees/ forest

This character is "Yong". It means eternity and contains the eight basic strokes of calligraphy.

The 8 basic movements needed to "construct this letter" are necessary if one is to be a calligrapher in Chinese.

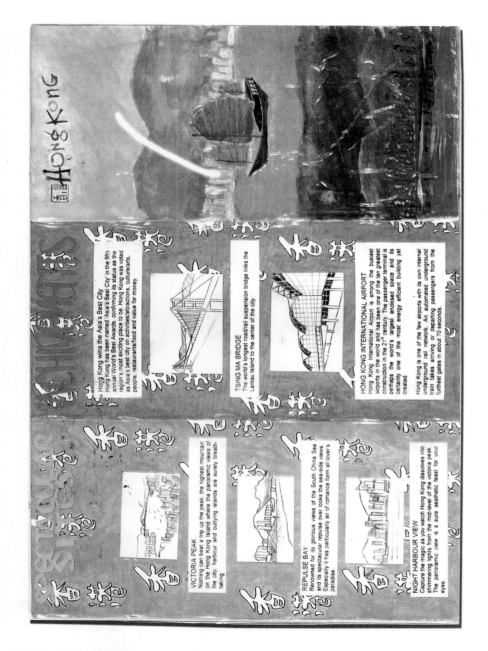

A brochure designed by a fifteen-year-old boy for Hong Kong, using both Chinese and Roman alphabet letters.

56

INTRODUCTION

Hong Kong, like a kaleidoscope, attracts worldwide interests for its extraordinary, intensely concentrated blend of oriental and occidental, of urban and rural, of nostalgic past and an aggressively modern present. This leaflet brings you to discover the city.

At the stroke of midnight on 30 June 1997, Hong Kong returned to China after 150 years of colonial rule, a historical event. Three years later, Hong Kong is a Special Administrative Region of China with a high degree of autonomy, operating under the unique arrangement known as "One Country, Two Systems". It retains its own legal, social and economic systems, which mean no change in lifestyle - for residents and visitors alike.

Today, Hong Kong is as vibrant as ever, bursting with life and dynamism. The calendar is overflowing with shows, events and festivals. Whole new dining districts are making the city streets come alive and people are out in force lapping up an almost hypnotic carnival atmosphere.

JUNK BOAT

HISTORIC SITES

TAI O VILLAGE
A neat fishing village situated on the northwestern coast of Lantau, with plenty of interesting and historic streets, traditional Chinese stilt-houses, small shops, stalls, shrines and temples.

FORMER YAMEN BUILDING KOWLOON WALLED CITY
The Yamen building, a three-hall structure was originally the administrative office of the Assistant Magistrate of Kowloon. In 1987, it was announced the Walled City would be cleared and replaced by a park.

PO LIN MONASTERY
The mountain peak echoes in the background of an ancient religion where it nests the exquisitely built monastery and the world's largest seated outdoor bronze Buddha.

SHOPPING

2ND FLOOR

TSIM SHA TSUI
Kowloon's numerous department stores and shopping centres, the superb harbour city with large shopping and entertainment complex is one of the largest and famous shopping mall in the area.

GOGO

CAUSEWAY BAY
World-class department stores from many countries have carved out a niche in Hong Kong. From the bastion of the British high street, Marks & Spencer, to Sogo of Japan, everything is available. Visit the popular Japanese-style emporiums, such as Seibu and Mitsukoshi.

SALE

STANLEY MARKET
Haunt of shopper heaven! Designers' fashion and casual wears are sold at reasonable prices. Besides, you will also find variety of merchandise like name chops, paintings, linen...etc

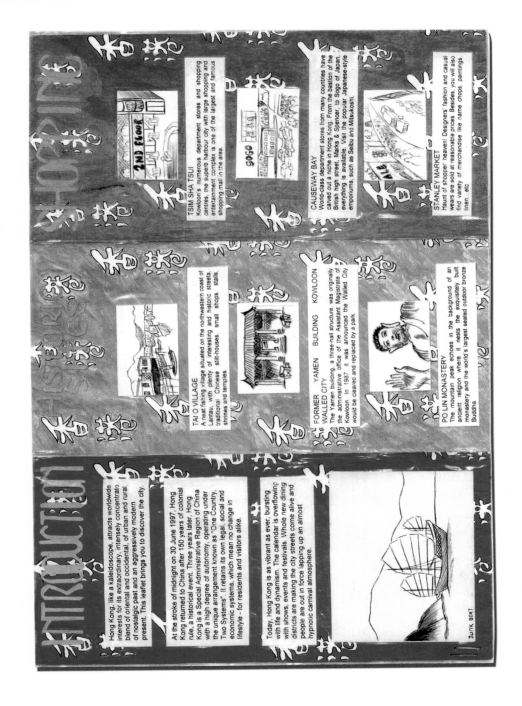

SEATED BUDDHA – fifth century

During the Gupta period, the Buddha became easily recognisable
by the oval face, serene smile, dreamy lotus eyes, elongated ears,
close-cropped ascetic's hair, slim body, and clinging light robe.

58

THE DEVANAGARI ALPHABET

THE BUDDHA'S EIGHTFOLD PATH:

1. Right understanding
2. Right thought
3. Right speech
4. Right action
5. Right livelihood
6. Right effort
7. Right mindfulness
8. Right concentration.

India's flag is one of symbolism:
Saffron stands for sacrifice and courage.
White stands for peace and truth.
Green stands for fertility and growth.

While the blue wheel (the Dharmachakra)
represents spiritual evolution.

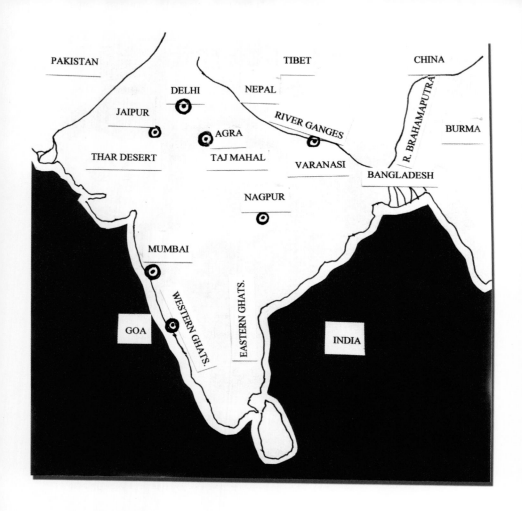

PAKISTAN

TIBET

CHINA

DELHI

NEPAL

JAIPUR

RIVER GANGES

AGRA

BURMA

THAR DESERT

TAJ MAHAL

VARANASI

R. BRAHAMAPUTRA

BANGLADESH

NAGPUR

MUMBAI

WESTERN GHATS.

EASTERN GHATS.

GOA

INDIA

Pattern from illustration in the Rasamanjari, painted in 1660–1670

THE DEVANĀGARĪ SCRIPT

अ	आ						
इ	ई	क	ख	ग	घ	ङ	
उ	ऊ	च	छ	ज	झ	ञ	
ऋ	ॠ	ट	ठ	ड	ढ	ण	
ए	ऐ	त	थ	द	ध	न	
ओ	औ	प	फ	ब	भ	म	

य	श
र	ष
ल	स
व	ह
ळ	
ड़	ढ़

TRANSLITERATION

a	ā						
i	ī	k	kh	g	gh	ṅ	
u	ū	c	ch	j	jh	ñ	
ṛ	ṝ	ṭ	ṭh	ḍ	ḍh	ṇ	
e	ai	t	th	d	dh	n	
o	au	p	ph	b	bh	m	

y	ś
r	ṣ
l	s
v	h
ḷ	
ṛ	ṁ

Hindi Equivalents of Roman Alphabets

A	–	अ	KH	–	ख़
Ā	–	आ	L	–	ल
T	–	Ă at end of a word अ	M	–	म
AI	–	ऐ, ै	Ṁ	–	ः
AU	–	औ, ौ	N	–	न
B	–	ब	Ṅ	–	ः
BH	–	भ	Ṇ	–	ण
C	–	च	O	–	ओ, ो
CH	–	छ	P	–	प
D	–	द	PH	–	फ
Ḍ	–	ड	Q	–	क़
DH	–	ढ	R	–	र
E	–	ए	Ṛ	–	ऋ, ृ
F	–	फ़	Ṛ	–	ड़
G	–	ग	RH	–	ढ़
Ġ	–	ग़	S	–	स
GH	–	घ	Ṣ	–	ष
H	–	ह	Ś	–	श
I	–	इ, ि	T	–	त
Ī	–	ई, ी	Ṭ	–	ट
J	–	ज	TH	–	ठ
JH	–	झ	TH	–	थ
J Ñ	–	ञ	U	–	उ., ु
K	–	क	U	–	ऊ, ू
KH	–	ख	V	–	व
KṢ	–	क्ष	Y	–	य
			Z	–	ज़

62

HOW TO WRITE
VOWELS & CONSONANTS

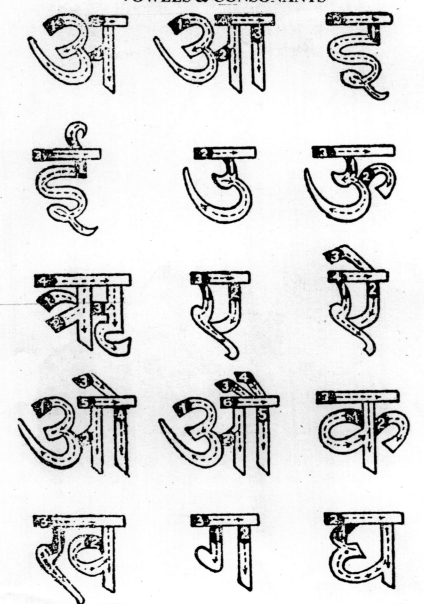

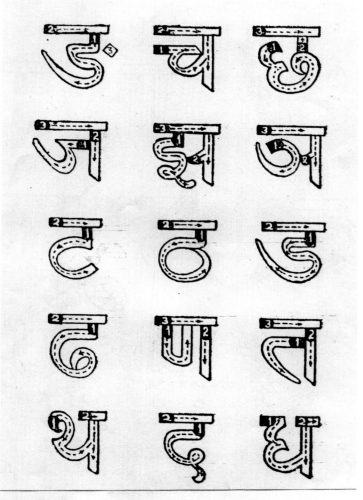

THE DEVANAGARI ALPHABET – SANSKRIT

There are many languages in India, a country which is approximately the size of Europe. As in Europe, there is a great variety of languages: Dravidian, Tamil, Vattshuttu, Kharoshthi, Urdu, Kaunada, Gujarati, Punjabi, Bengali, to name but a few.

What the Roman alphabet is to a lot of the European languages, Sanskrit is to India. The Sanskrit alphabet can be traced back to roughly 1500 B.C. and the word "Sanskrit", translated, roughly means "polished, refined, perfected".

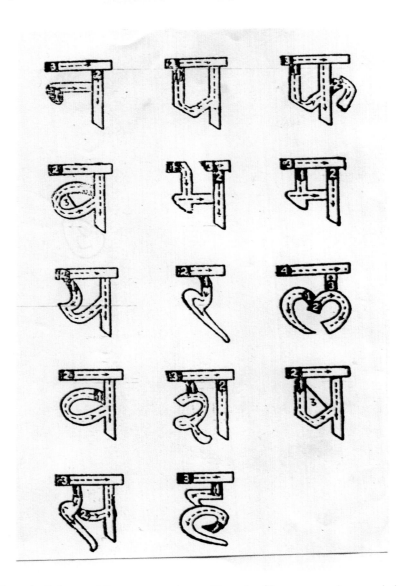

Sanskrit is most commonly written in Devanagari, an alphabet consisting of 48 letters. It is written from left to right. As with other south Asian scripts, the letters appear to hang from the line. This immediately contrasts with the Roman alphabet, which is written above the line. The line of Devanagari is actually a component part of the letters and is drawn as the writing moves.

Prior to independence in 1947, Hindi and Urdu were referred to as Hindustani.

Hinduism means "right living" or dharma, and spiritual development in life.

English words of Hindi origin are: lot, look, thug, chintz, dungaree, pundit, chutney, tom-tom, and juggernaut, to name a few.

PROJECTS – PRACTICAL WORK

Ideas and suggestions for practical work

How the Devanagari alphabet can be used by you:

- Devanagari letters can give the impression of a distorted figure. Make the letters enact the figures, and the figures will become the letters.
- A poster – for a sports meeting – people in action.
- A medical display – figures expressing and enacting medical terms.

The examples shown will give you ideas as to what you can do.

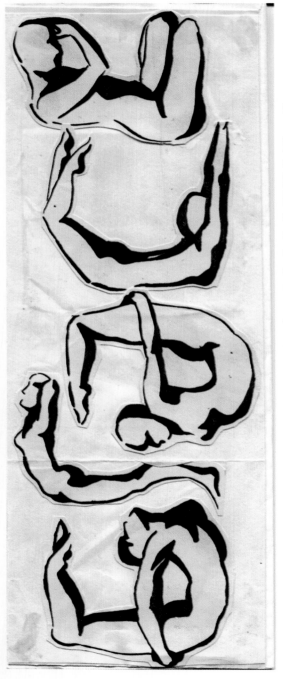

GRACE

– onomatopoeia – Devanagari-type letters enact what the word is saying. Each letter is isolated, in that it is an entity in itself. However, each letter in the shape of a human being plays a role which together makes the whole word.

Draw up a letter/ figure, contrasting thick and thin lines. Complete in black ink or paint.

HEBREW LETTERS OF SYMMETRY

The word "Bible" comes from the Greek word "biblia", meaning "books", which in turn comes from "Byblos" meaning "Papyrus", the material from which the books were made.

The New Testament, the last part of the Bible to be written in the first century A.D., was written on sheets of paper made from papyrus.

The Bible was first printed in English in 1525.

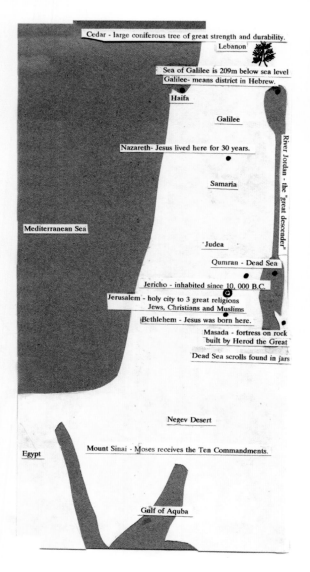

Cedar - large coniferous tree of great strength and durability.

Lebanon

Sea of Galilee is 209m below sea level
Galilee- means district in Hebrew.

Haifa

Galilee

Nazareth- Jesus lived here for 30 years.

Samaria

River Jordan - the "great descender"

Mediterranean Sea

Judea

Qumran - Dead Sea

Jericho - inhabited since 10, 000 B.C.

Jerusalem - holy city to 3 great religions
Jews, Christians and Muslims

Bethlehem - Jesus was born here.

Masada - fortress on rock
built by Herod the Great

Dead Sea scrolls found in jars

Negev Desert

Egypt

Mount Sinai - Moses receives the Ten Commandments.

Gulf of Aquba

The six-pointed star – the symbol of Judaism.

THE HEBREW ALPHABET

aleph	beth	gimel	daleth
he	van	zayih	cheth
teth	yod	kaph	iamed
mem	nun	samekh	ayin
pe	tsade	gaph	resh
shin	tau		

THE DEVELOPMENT OF VARIOUS ALPHABETS IN ANCIENT PALESTINE

Proto-Sinaitic circa. 1500 B.C.	Phoenician circa. 1000 B.C.	Early Hebrew circa. 586 B.C.

Proto-Sinaitic circa. 1500 B.C.

- ꖴ OX
- HOUSE
- THROW STICK
- FISH
- MAN WITH ARMS RAISED
- WEAPON
- PALM OF HAND
- WATER
- SNAKE
- EYE
- MOUTH
- PLANT
- MONKEY
- HEAD
- CROSS MARK

ISRAEL

ayin tzadeh
pe peh
tsadet tzadeh
goph kohf
resh reysh
shin shin
tau tav

HEBREW
22 letters

aleph aleph
beth bet
gimel gimel
daleth dalet
he heh
van vav
zayin zayin
cheth chet
teth tet
yod yud
kaph kaf
lamed lamed
mem mem
nun nun
samekh samekh

The Hebrew alphabet consists of only 22 consonants and is read from right to left on a straight line.

Hebrew letters have not changed since the Hebrew alphabet developed from Aramaic in the 2nd century B.C.

WAYS WITH HEBREW

If you turn around some of the old Hebrew letters, you will see they are almost identical to English letters.

Here are some examples:

- ⚡ is old Hebrew א. Set it upright; it is an A.
- ◁ is old Hebrew ר. Turn it sideways and curve it slightly;
     it is a D.
- ⅂ is old Hebrew ה. Turn it round and it is an E.
- ᙏ is old Hebrew רנ. It resembles M.
- w is old Hebrew ש. Turn it sideways and curve the line,
     and it will be an S.

"Amen"

In this word, the Hebrews expressed their every wish and hope. God would look on them favourably and grant them all they wanted.

From Hebrew the word spread to over a thousand languages. It has entered into more languages and is used in more countries than any other word.

Many common words and
phrases in English come
originally from the Bible:

The fat of the land	(Gen. 45:18)
Eat, drink and be merry	(Eccles. 8:15)
A leopard cannot change its spots	(Jer. 13:23)
The straight and narrow	(Matt. 7:14)
A wolf in sheep's clothing	(Matt. 7:15)
A thorn in the flesh	(2 Cor. 12:17)

	Name	Phonetic value
א	alef	[ʔ]
ב	beys	[b, v]
ג	gimel	[g]
ד	daled	[d]
ה	hey	[h, ʔ]
ו	vov	[v]
ז	zayen	[z]
ח	khes	[x]
ט	tes	[t]
י	yud	[j]
כ, ך	khaf	[k, x]
ל	lamed	[l]
מ, ם	mem	[m]
נ, ן	nun	[n]
ס	samekh	[s]
ע	ayen	[ʔ]
פ, ף	pey	[p, f]
צ, ץ	tsadi	[ts]
ק	kuf	[k]
ר	reysh	[ʁ]
ש	shin	[ʃ, s]
ת	tov	[t, s]

The Bible is a whole library – there are sixty-six books in it. There are two parts to the Bible: the Old Testament or Covenant, and the New Testament.

The Old Testament tells of God's choice of the Hebrews, through Abraham, to be his people, and the way by which He led them to become a great nation and taught them to worship Him, so that they might make Him known to all other people.

The New Testament tells how God came Himself, in the person of Jesus Christ, to show men what He is like and how He wants to be served. He tells, too, of how his followers went out into the world to tell the Good News of Jesus to everyone who would listen.

It was in Egypt, under the Greek reigning monarch Ptolemy II, that the Hebrew people were encouraged to make copies of their writings in Greek, which most of them understood.

The New Testament was written in Greek. Like the Old Testament, it was originally a number of separate writings known as the New Writings. It was not until after the third century after Christ that all these new writings were collected and made into one book.

Here is the Hebrew word which stands for the first three words of the Bible – "In the beginning" (this is how it would be written in English) – without any spaces between the words. The small dots beside certain letters are "points" or vowels. Early Hebrew writing did not have the points.

This letter ❯ is called "yod" and it is the smallest letter in the Hebrew alphabet. Jesus referred to this sign to show the everlasting nature of God's word (Matt. 5:18).

The beautiful letters of the Hebrew alphabet are to be found in the Hebrew Scriptures. "Scripture" means a writing, and these are the sacred writings of the Hebrew people. They are known today as the Old Testament and originally each book was written on a separate roll, and they are still read in this form in the Jewish Synagogues.

PROJECTS – PRACTICAL WORK

Ideas and suggestions for practical work
How the Hebrew alphabet can be used by you:
- Hebrew-type letters go well with faces and heads as they are so expressive, and their square shape re-echoes that subject.
- Faces – human emotions: happiness, sadness, anger, surprise etc.
- Maps – where subject matter and letters are entwined.
- Illustration – art work with a religious character.
- Perspective – bold letters advancing towards and receding from you.

Materials
Pencils, measuring tools, coloured pencils, inks and brushes.
These examples shown will give you ideas as to what to do.

Faces re-echo square-type letters. Human emotion based on the contours of the face: A, attractive; G, glum etc. Form and depth are implied by concentrating the letters closely together or spacing them widely apart.

PROJECTS

PROPORTION "TYPEFACE"

In this example, letters are in proportion to height so as to create a sense of drama.

Draw up simple block-type letters which accentuate perspective and 3-D form.

Although the letters are static, a feeling of movement is implied by the diagonal stripes in various colours.

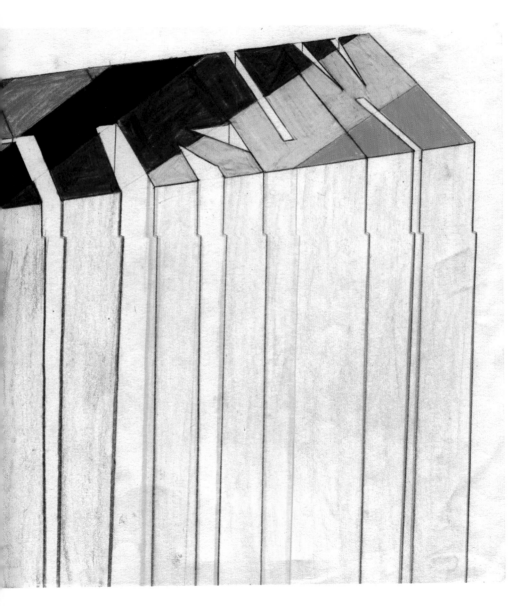

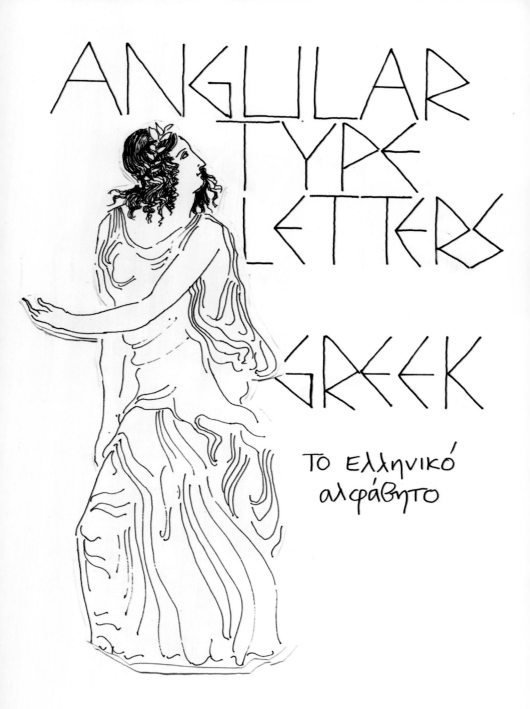

ANGULAR
TYPE
LETTERS

GREEK

ΤΟ Ελληνικό
αλφάβητο

80

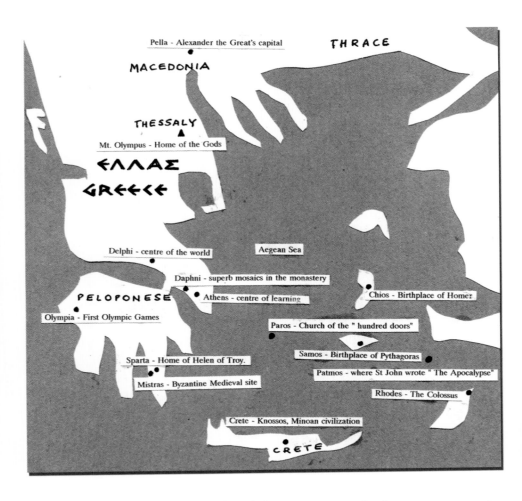

Pella - Alexander the Great's capital

THRACE

MACEDONIA

THESSALY

Mt. Olympus - Home of the Gods

ΕΛΛΑΣ

GREECE

Delphi - centre of the world

Aegean Sea

Daphni - superb mosaics in the monastery

PELOPONESE   Athens - centre of learning

Chios - Birthplace of Homer

Olympia - First Olympic Games

Paros - Church of the " hundred doors"

Samos - Birthplace of Pythagoras

Sparta - Home of Helen of Troy.

Patmos - where St John wrote " The Apocalypse"

Mistras - Byzantine Medieval site

Rhodes - The Colossus

Crete - Knossos, Minoan civilization

CRETE

Centres in Greece in which Greek letters as angular forms appear on buildings, churches, icons, frescoes, and museums.

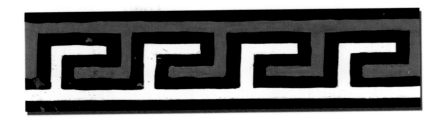

THE GREEK ALPHABET

The Greek alphabet has developed over a long period of time. So long, in fact, that it is thought that there were as many as a dozen Greek alphabets or, rather, variations on the original Phoenician from which it evolved.

Although several letters of the Phoenician alphabet are similar to Greek, the fact remains that Phoenician was written from right to left (as are Arabic and Hebrew) and Greek from left to right. Even so, early Greek followed the course of the plough going from right to left, left to right, then right to left in turn, as a farmer does when ploughing his field ("boustrophedon" as mentioned earlier).

It was a momentous occasion for Europe when the Greeks decided to write from left to right, and to continue every sentence each time beginning on the left.

The Greeks thus adopted the left to right direction and evolved an elegant, clear, logical, legible form of capital letters for inscription on stone and pottery. Lower-case letters are really a development of hastily written capitals, which was the only form of writing the Greeks themselves knew before the seventh century A.D.

Logic and proportion, inherent constituents in the formation of Greek letters, are to be found in all their creations. They believed that the artist realises in his work not a copy of nature, but its laws of structure. The proportions of the golden section, i.e. the division of a distance or a mass into two parts, the lesser of which is to the greater, as the largest part is to the total length or whole. The phenomena of proportion as expressed in the measurements of the human body; in the distance between the rows of branches in a young fir tree which taper to the top; in the measurements of the egg shape, or in the spiral of a snail shell – to mention a few examples – always revealed the proportions of the golden mean.

THE GREEK ALPHABET

Αα	Ββ	Γγ	Δδ
alpha	vita	gamma	delta
Εε	Ζζ	Ηη	Θθ
epsilon	zita	ita	thita
Ιι	Κκ	Λλ	Μμ
iota	kapa	lamda	mi
Νν	Ξξ	Οο	Ππ
ni	ksi	omikron	pi
Ρρ	Σσς	Ττ	Υυ
ro	sigma	taf	ipsilon
Φφ	Χχ	Ψψ	Ωω
fi	hi	psi	omega

ΓΡΑΜΜΑΤΑ ΜΑΘΕΙΝ ΔΕΙ ΚΑΙ ΜΑΘΟΝΤΑ ΝΟΥΝ ΕΧΕΙΝ –

It is necessary to learn letters and having learnt them, to have good sense.

Menander
Greek Dramatist
(342–291 B.C.)

GREEK
24 letters

Α α alpha	Ν ν nu
Β β beta	Ξ ξ xi
Γ γ gamma	Ο ο omicron
Δ δ delta	Π π pi
Ε ε epsilon	Ρ ρ rho
Ζ ζ zeta	Σ ς sigma
Η η eta	Τ τ tau
Θ θ theta	Υ υ epsilon
Ι ι iota	Φ φ phi
Κ κ kappa	Χ χ chi
Λ λ lambda	Ψ ψ psi
Μ μ mu	Ω ω omega

Greek influences English in many ways, some examples of which follow:

Alpha – Omega (the First and the Last): $A - \Omega$

Area of a circle: Πr^2

Words derived from Greek, such as Philip, philosophy, and telephone, have the F sound in English: Φ (PH)

Words beginning with these letters, such as psychic, psychology, and pseudonym, are usually pronounced as if they begin with S: Ψ (PS)

Gamma rays (X-rays of very short wavelength emitted by radioactive substances): Γ (G)

"I don't care one iota. Do it!": I (i)

This is Greek and how they spelt her:
Alpha, Beta, Gamma, Delta,
Epsilon, Zeta, Eta, Theta,
then Iota, Kappa too, followed up by Lambda, Mu, Nu, Xi,
Omikron, Pi
after that Rho, Sigma, Tau, Upsilon, Phi,
and still three more: Chi, Psi and Omega – which is twenty-four.

The Stele on which the text was engraved was placed, in antiquity, in the temple of Olympic Zeus.

The Palmette (Latin 'palma', a hand)

The principle, a series of fan-like features connected by scrolls, is to be found in most historical styles.

natural acanthus

acanthus

dolphin

Christ Pantocrator in the dome of the eleventh century Byzantine monastery at Daphni. The letters stand for IC (Jesus) and XP (Christ) in Greek.

The first two letters of the name of Christ are sometimes seen in churches as this monogram:

Phenomena of Proportion

Out of this concern with scale arose the ideal human body as portrayed in Greek sculptures. Harmonious results were obtained in pottery where the golden mean was applied, and in temple buildings too, where all parts of the construction bear an understanding of proportion based on logical calculation.

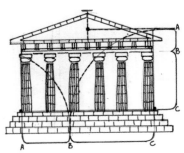

Front view of a Greek Doric temple showing the proportion of the golden mean.

A. Branches taper to top.
B. Spacing between branches diminishes towards the top.

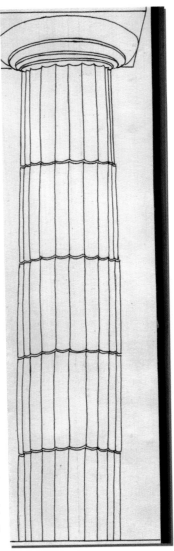

The heritage of Greece is still present in our writing today:

Mathematical symbols are based on Greek letters.

The Greek alphabet is the basis of Russian, Cyrillic (Serbian, Bulgarian) as well as the Roman alphabet.

It is an essential part of any Orthodox icon.

Increasingly, scientific words use Greek letters and words; in fact, Greek is the fastest-growing language in English today.

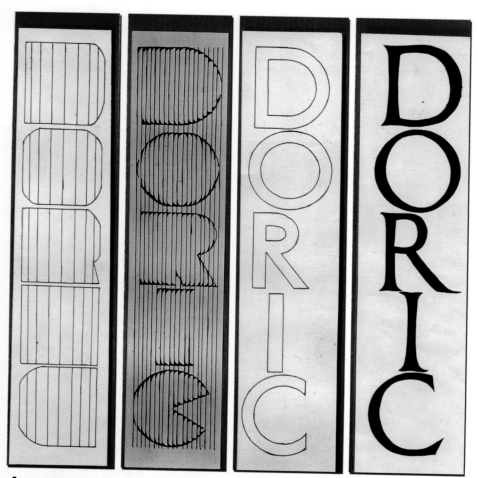

An example of TRANSFORMATION using Angular Forms.

Although the word DORIC uses Roman letters, the idea comes from a Greek column, one of the three orders of architecture, i.e. Doric, Ionic, and Corinthian.

Greek letters are a combination of masculine shapes, i.e. angular or architectural, and feminine, i.e. organic. Most of the letters are angular, reflecting the position of men in society in ancient times.

ΑΓΔΕΖΗΙΚΛΜΝΞΠΣΤΥΧ

PROJECTS – PRACTICAL WORK

Ideas and suggestions for practical work

How the Greek alphabet can be used by you:

- Greek letters are angular and architectural in character.
- Poster – draw attention to mathematical principles by using Greek.
- Self-portrait – using your name in Greek and Roman letters.
- An icon – paint yourself an icon for your Name Day and include your name.
- Palindrome – palindromes can be the basis for so many designs.
- Greek words in English – theme (ΘΕΜΑ), drama (ΔΡΑΜΑ), catastrophe (ΚΑΤΑΣΤΡΟΦΗ), orchestra (ΟΡΧΗΣΤΡΑ) etc.

Materials

The above can be carried out in a variety of media – gold paint could be particularly useful.

The examples shown will give you ideas as to what to do.

Author's work inspired by Greek letters.

Programme cover by a 16-year-old student – letters reflect strength of the subject and are an adaptation of ancient Greek drama.

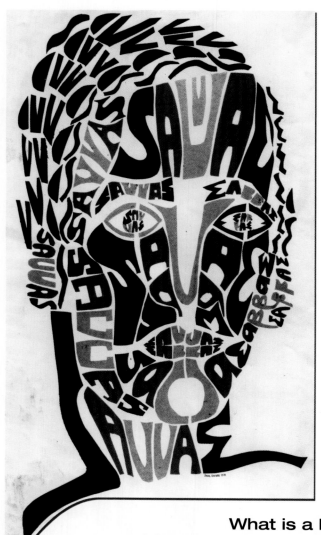

What is a PALINDROME?

It is a statement or word that reads identically backwards and forwards.

SAVVAS, the author's surname, is a palindrome. Letters from both Greek and Roman alphabets have been used to create a self-portrait.

Other palindromes include: Anna, Abba, level, rotator, refer, madam, Malayalam (the language of Kerala, India.), pop, pip, poop, gig, gag. Rats live on no evil star.

Characters
of rhythm
and
harmony

THE
ROMAN
ALPHABET

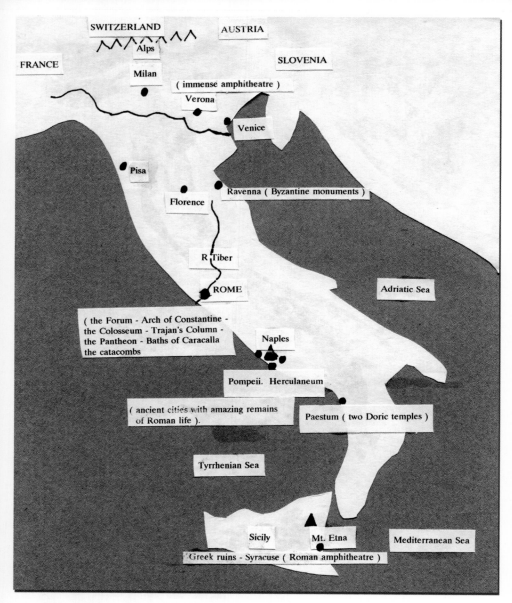

SWITZERLAND
AUSTRIA
Alps
FRANCE
SLOVENIA
Milan
(immense amphitheatre)
Verona
Venice
Pisa
Ravenna (Byzantine monuments)
Florence
R. Tiber
ROME
Adriatic Sea
(the Forum - Arch of Constantine -
the Colosseum - Trajan's Column -
the Pantheon - Baths of Caracalla
the catacombs
Naples
Pompeii. Herculaneum
(ancient cities with amazing remains
of Roman life).
Paestum (two Doric temples)
Tyrrhenian Sea
Sicily
Mt. Etna
Mediterranean Sea
Greek ruins - Syracuse (Roman amphitheatre)

Italian design, second century A.D.

94

THE ROMAN ALPHABET

The Roman alphabet, like much of Roman culture, had its origins in the centuries of commercial and intellectual trade among diverse Mediterranean countries.

Concepts and symbols came from the Greeks. The traditional culture of the Greeks was still alive in the art of the first century and so one can see the way to approach the harmonious forms of the Roman capital script. As Roman power grew and spread, the alphabet became an essential tool for maintaining the Empire.

In addition to its beauty, simplicity, and clarity, the Roman letter showed from its very beginnings the quality of resilience. It is very easy to write and read in many different media, in many different sizes, and it communicates clearly whether written with a small pen or carved in stone letters, however tall.

On the next page, the map shows the Roman Empire at the time when it was at its greatest extent. Like all great empires of the past, it eventually collapsed, but it had lasted four hundred years. In spite of the chaos that followed the fall of Rome, much of Roman civilisation remains today. Roman roads were the highways of Europe for 1,500 years after Rome fell.

Every day, Roman letters are used in writing. Missionaries from Rome brought Christianity to the British Isles. The letters of the English alphabet came from the Roman alphabet although the Romans did not have J, U and W.

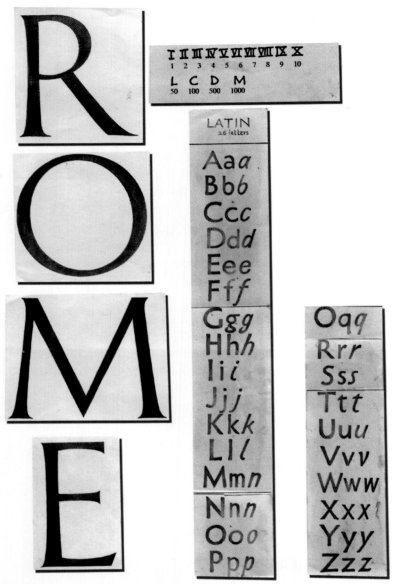

ROME

I	II	III	IV	V	VI	VII	VIII	IX	X
1	2	3	4	5	6	7	8	9	10

L	C	D	M
50	100	500	1000

LATIN
26 letters

Aaa
Bbb
Ccc
Ddd
Eee
Fff
Ggg
Hhh
Iii
Jjj
Kkk
Lll
Mmn
Nnn
Ooo
Ppp

Oqq
Rrr
Sss
Ttt
Uuu
Vvv
Www
Xxx
Yyy
Zzz

Roman letters are only rarely used as numbers. Arabic figures (1, 2, 3...) are far more commonly used.

The Latin script which is always read from left to right has capital (majuscule) and small, or lower, case letters (miniscule).

The Roman Empire in the time of Trajan, 98–117 A.D.

The stamp of Roman culture influenced European civilisation in many ways, one of the most important being the Roman alphabet. Though the original Latin alphabet consisted of 24 letters, two have since been added: J and W.

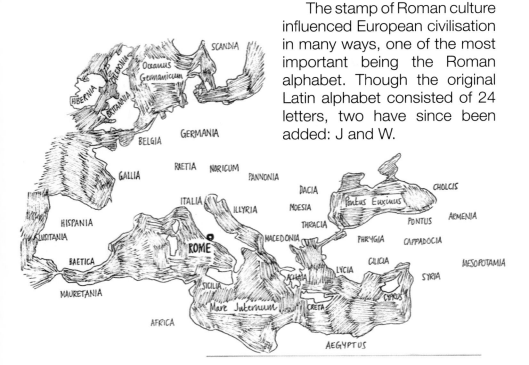

Arch of Constantine, Rome, 312 A.D. Roman Corinthian. The beauty of incised Roman capitals is clearly visible on one of the great triumphal arches of Rome.

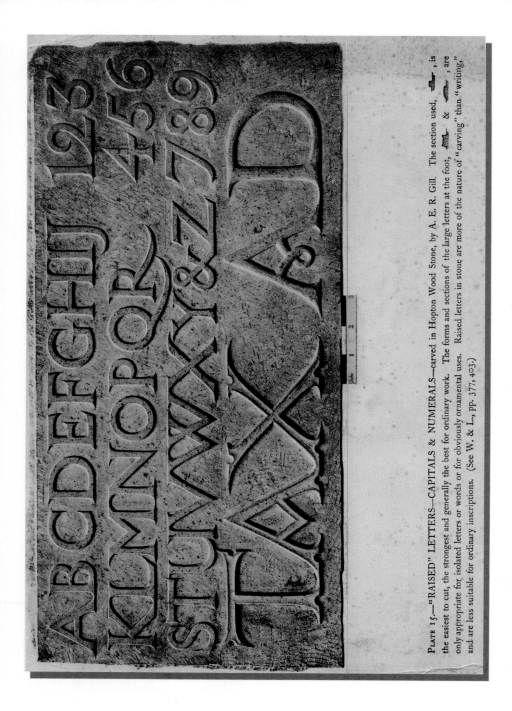

PLATE 15.—"RAISED" LETTERS—CAPITALS & NUMERALS—carved in Hopton Wood Stone, by A. E. R. Gill. The section used, ⬤, is the easiest to cut, the strongest and generally the best for ordinary work. The forms and sections of the large letters at the foot, ⬤ & ⬤, are only appropriate for isolated letters or words or for obviously ornamental uses. Raised letters in stone are more of the nature of "carving" than "writing," and are less suitable for ordinary inscriptions. (See W. & L., pp. 377, 403.)

Spacing

Spacing is an important element of design in letter forms. The aim in spacing is to create a general effect of evenness and to avoid the feeling of being "spread out", or cramped. In general, the following should be remembered:

The space between two straight verticals should be greater than that between a vertical line and a curve, e.g. H N; H C; or two open letters, e.g. F S.

Two curved letters – e.g., D Q, or a straight line and a projecting line, e.g. R L – should be placed rather more closely together.

The "white shapes", the negative spaces inside the letters, around the letters, and between letters in a word, are as visually important as the black strokes themselves. Learn to judge the area, not the linear distance between the letters and words.

The ability to draw good letters efficiently is not good enough; there must also be the ability to put the letters together to form words. Letters, however beautiful in themselves, must be arranged very carefully when formed into words or else they are of little value.

Proportions and design elements in Roman letters. The relationship between height and width of each letter.

E F L B P R S

E F L B P R S – half as wide as they are tall.

H T U K N

H T U K N A V X Z – about ¾ as wide as they are tall.

M W I J

M W – about 25% wider than they are tall.   I J – very narrow letters

E B S X

E B S X – have a smaller top than bottom.

F P R A Y – cross below the exact centre line.

F P R A Y – also have a smaller bottom than top.

O C G Q D – are exactly as wide as they are tall.

A V X Y Z – it is the contrast between these wide and narrow letters that gives character and beauty to the finished word.

H – horizontal slightly above geometrical middle.

F P R – are identical on the left hand 1/3 of the letter.

E B L D – similarly share the same backs.

A is an inverted V.   M W – both are contained in midsection.

PROJECTS – PRACTICAL WORK

Ideas and suggestions for practical work

How the Roman alphabet can be used by you:

- Experiment with the pattern shapes and spaces between and around the letters.
- Design a Roman capital letter with entasis and serifs. Paint positive/negative parts in complementary colours.
- O and C – make an interlocking O and C, or use your own initials.
- Fashion – design your own clothes for a summer collection, printing a letter design on your chosen material.

Materials

The above can be carried out in a variety of media, and these include lino blocks, fabrics, and different papers including cellophane.

The examples shown will give you ideas as to what you can do.

LETTER CONSTRUCTION

How to draw a Roman capital 'A' with entasis and serifs.

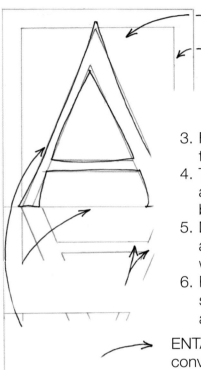

1. Measure up a piece of cartridge paper, 220mm x 100mm (or according to personal requirements).
2. Draw a border all the way round and divide the paper in half.
3. Find the middle and draw two Vs back to back.
4. The left and middle "thick" bars of both are the same width – the wide bars of both letters are roughly the same.
5. Draw the lines with entasis freehand, as a Roman sculpture or calligrapher would have done.
6. Paint the two As, and the negative spaces around and between, in alternate colours.

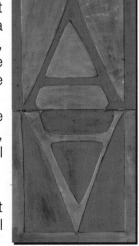

ENTASIS – a slight convex curve in a column or vertical line, so as to correct the visual illusion that the straight lines give of curving upwards.

It entails curving the lines slightly to make the lines more pleasing to the eye. Without entasis, the letters would appear to have a mechanical stiffness.

SERIFS should be carefully drawn and not exaggerated, otherwise a "fish-tail" effect will be the result. Serifs "finish the letter off".

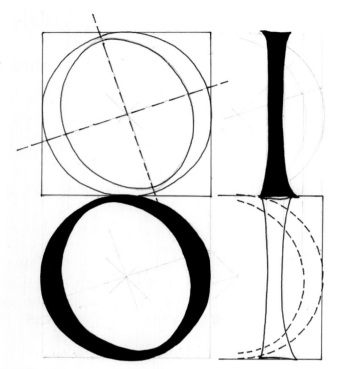

O and I are the two basic "shapes" on which all the Roman letters are based. Each letter is either angular (masculine), i.e. A E F H I K L M N T V W X Y Z, or organic (feminine), i.e. C O Q S, or a combination of both, i.e. B D G J P R U.

The tendency in the letter is for the straight lines to be horizontal and vertical, and for the round letters to be circular.

The Letter O

1. Draw a square.
2. Draw a circle in the square.
3. Divide each of the four sides into 1/3 – 2/3.
4. Draw two arcs/curves inside the O as shown.
5. Round off the top and bottom with freehand-drawn lines.
6. Note that the inside arcs/curves of the Roman O are tilted.

I is drawn using the O as a basis. Note that the left-hand side of the top serif and the right-hand side of the bottom serif are slightly bigger.

**R O M A N
ALPHABET.**
Experimenting
with   pattern
shapes   through
colour.

BASIC DESIGN VALUES IN THE ROMAN ALPHABET

- Architectural, masculine letters based on angles. They are made up of vertical, horizontal and diagonal lines:

A E F H I K L M N T V W X Y Z

- Organic, feminine letters based on round forms:

C O Q S

- Letters which combine design values of both:

B D G J P R U

- Wide letters:

A C D G H M N O Q T W X Z

- Medium width letters:

B E F K L P R S U V Y

- Narrow letters:

I J

When you look at other letters in other alphabets which are less familiar to you, try to see similar design values in them that you already know in your own.

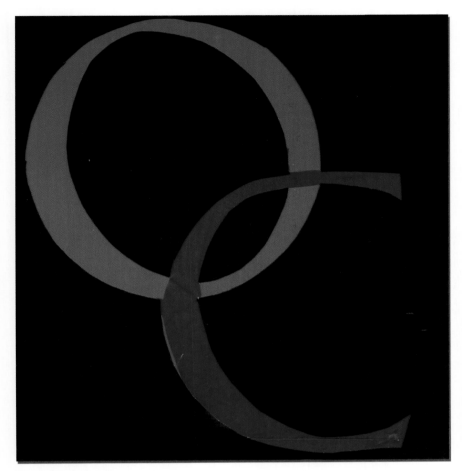

The letters O and C

1. Draw two Os as previously.
2. Interlock the two Os and convert the second one into a C.
3. Cut out the O and C (black card in the example) taking care not to lose the small oval piece between the two letters.
4. The basic colour (blue card in the example) in the form of the two letters now shows through.
5. Place the transparent papers (yellow cellophane in the example) to shape the C.

You need two contrasting colours and a transparent paper such as cellophane or tissue paper so as to make an interesting overprint.

FLAKE.
By 15-year-old student using coloured pencils and charcoal.

108

ARABIC

The Running Script

THE ARABIC ALPHABET

The Arabic alphabet and language is in daily use by 200 million people.

Arabic is the language of daily communication in Egypt, Libya, Tunisia, Algeria, Morocco, Western Sahara, Sudan, Somalia, Saudi Arabia, Yemen, Syria, Iraq, Lebanon, Jordan, Kuwait, Oman, Qatar, Bahrain, and United Arab Emirates.

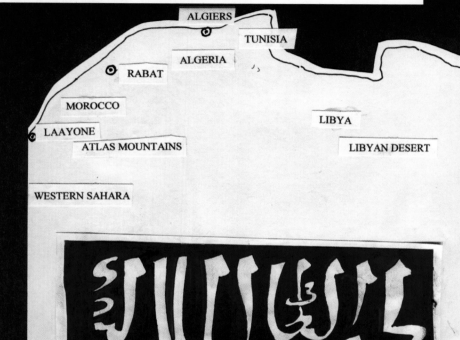

ALGIERS

TUNISIA

ALGERIA

RABAT

MOROCCO

LIBYA

LAAYONE

ATLAS MOUNTAINS

LIBYAN DESERT

WESTERN SAHARA

MECCA – MEDINA – BASRA – KUFA

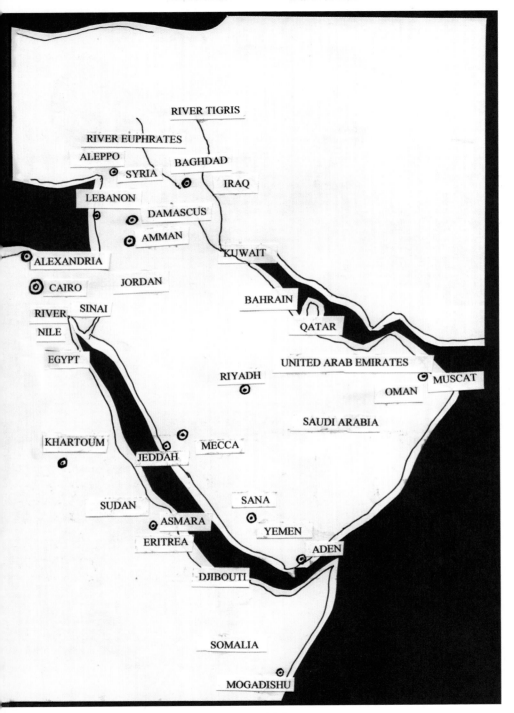

RIVER TIGRIS

RIVER EUPHRATES

ALEPPO

BAGHDAD

SYRIA

IRAQ

LEBANON

DAMASCUS

AMMAN

ALEXANDRIA

KUWAIT

CAIRO

JORDAN

BAHRAIN

RIVER

SINAI

QATAR

NILE

EGYPT

UNITED ARAB EMIRATES

RIYADH

MUSCAT

OMAN

SAUDI ARABIA

KHARTOUM

MECCA

JEDDAH

SUDAN

SANA

ASMARA

YEMEN

ERITREA

ADEN

DJIBOUTI

SOMALIA

MOGADISHU

111

alif	baa'	taa'	thaa'
jiim	Haa'	khaa'	daal
dhaal	raa'	zaay	siin
shiin	Saad	Daad	Taa'
Dhaa'	iayn	ghayn	faa'
qaaf	kaaf	laam	miim
nuun	haa'	waaw	yaa'

3

MEMBERS OF THE ARAB LEAGUE جَامِعَةُ الدُّوَلِ العَرَبِيَّةِ

العاصمة	Capital	البلد	Country
الجزائر	Algiers	الجزائر	Algeria
المنامة	Manama	البحرين	Bahrain
موروني	Moroni	جزر القمر	Comoros
جيبوتي	Djibouti	جيبوتي	Djibouti
القاهرة	Cairo	مصر	Egypt
بغداد	Baghdad	العراق	Iraq
عمّان	Amman	الأردن	Jordan
الكويت	Kuwait City	الكويت	Kuwait
بيروت	Beirut	لبنان	Lebanon
طرابلس	Tripoli	ليبيا	Libya
نواكشوط	Nouakchott	موريتانيا	Mauritania
الرباط	Rabat	المغرب	Morocco
مسقط	Musqat	عُمان	Oman
القدس*	Jerusalem*	فلسطين	Palestine
دوحة	Doha	قطر	Qatar
الرياض	Riyadh	المملكة العربية السعودية	Kingdom of Saudi Arabia
مقديشو	Mogadishu	الصومال	Somalia
الخرطوم	Khartoum	السودان	Sudan
دمشق	Damascus	سوريا	Syria
تونس	Tunis	تونس	Tunisia
أبو ظبي	Abu Dhabi	الإمارات العربية المتّحدة	United Arab Emirates:
		أبو ظبي	*Abu Dhabi*
		عجمان	*Ajman*
		دبيّ	*Dubai*
		الفجيرة	*Fujairah*
		رأس الخيمة	*Ras al-Khaimah*
		الشارقة	*Sharjah*
		أمّ القيوين	*Umm al-Qaiwain*
صنعاء	San'a	اليمن	Yemen

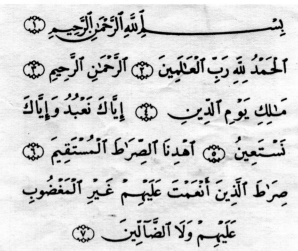

The above is the opening chapter of the Koran:

1. In the name of Allah, the Beneficent, the Merciful.
2. Praise be to Allah, the Lord of the Worlds.
3. The Beneficent, the Merciful.
4. Master of the Day of Judgement.
5. Thee (alone) do we worship, and thee (alone) we ask for help.
6. Show us the straight path.
7. The path of those whom thou hast favoured; not (the path) of those who earn thy anger nor of those who go astray.

ARABIC
28 letters

ا	alif
ب	bā
ت	tā
ث	thā
ج	jīm
ح	hā
خ	khā
د	dāl
ذ	dhāl
ر	rā
ز	zā
س	sīn
ش	shīn
ص	sād
ض	dād
ط	tā
ظ	zā
ع	'ain
غ	ghain
ف	fā
ق	kāf
ك	kāf
ل	lām
م	mīm
ن	nūn
ه	hā
و	waw
ي	ya

Arabic is written with 28 letters and is read from right to left on a horizontal line.

The earliest inscriptions of Arabic date back to the fourth century. Broadly speaking, each letter represents one consonant of the Arabic language, and each consonant is represented by exactly one letter. The importance of calligraphy in Islamic art is without parallel in almost any other culture.

Several styles of calligraphy developed, from earliest times which are used in books, but also from the essential elements in architecture.

The Holy Koran expressly forbids the visual representation of the human form and thus artists were encouraged to express themselves through the creative use of Arabic letter forms. In fact, letter forms adorned almost everything in the Muslim world: books, icons, coins, ceramics, buildings, carpets. Calligraphers in the Islamic world are highly thought of.

Koran means "recitation" and the Koran declares that God taught by the pen. Learning the word of God by carefully reciting and accurate copying is the basis of traditional education.

My pen works miracles and rightly enough is the form
of my words and proud of its superiority and meaning.
To each of the curves of any letters, the heavenly vault
confesses its bondage in slavery. The value of each of my
strokes is eternity itself.
So wrote the Persian calligrapher Mullah Mir Ali.

The alphabet and written language has remained remarkably constant since the sixth century A.D., mainly because of the unifying influence of the Koran.

FACTS

- Arabic: "The flowing script".
- The Arabic alphabet has no capital letters.
- Words are written in joined-up writing.
- Dots appear over or under the script.
- They are added after the main word has been completed.
- The Arabic alphabet and written language has remained remarkably constant for 1,400 years, due largely to the unifying factor of the Koran.
- In 1974, Arabic was made the sixth official language of the United Nations.

Arabic words in English include: Algebra, alcohol, alcove, albatross, mosque, minaret, sultan, haven, giraffe, cotton, amber, sofa, mattress, tariff, magazine, arsenal, syrup, artichoke and, of course, coffee.

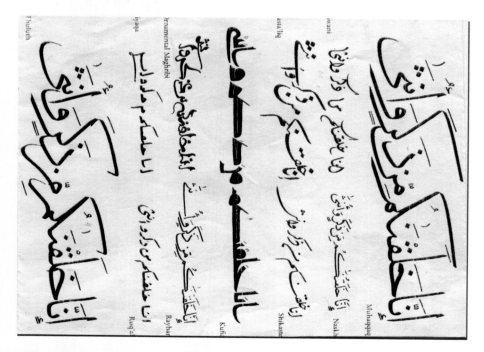

A Koranic passage in a variety of calligraphic styles.

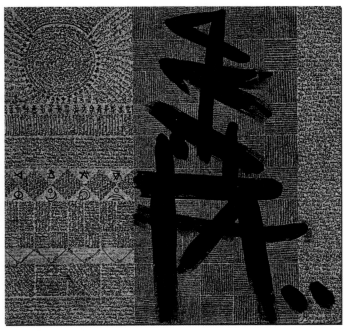

How Arabic has inspired painting in the western world

An example of the work by the Swiss painter and etcher Paul Klee (1879–1940), whose linear style recalls Arabic letters. Although Klee was closely associated with the German Expressionists, particularly Der Blaue Reiter and especially Kandinsky and Jawlensky, he was very much an individual artist who strongly advocated work being allowed to grow and develop, such as "taking a line for a walk". All sorts of fantastic images could be developed and compounded.

PROJECTS – PRACTICAL WORK

Ideas and suggestions for practical work
How the Arabic alphabet can be used by you:
- Arabic-type script can be used to make flowing repetitive lines which create movement.
- Line making – make different lines of varying thicknesses, e.g. "go for a walk".
- Role play – make letters do what they are saying, such as run, skip, panic, jump, crawl, fly, dance.
- Tiles – design tiles based on abstract, geometric shapes using Arabic in rich colours.

Materials
The above can be carried out in a variety of media, but also including string.

    The examples shown will give you ideas as to what you can do.

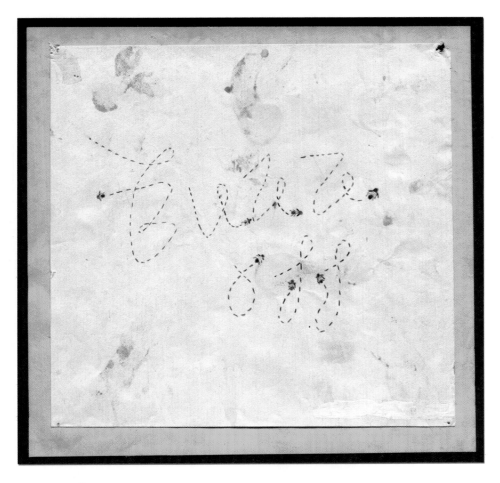

BUZZ OFF.
14-year-old needlework/pencil – free interpretation of a bee's movements in space.

Taking a line for a walk – the dotted line here is very effective. There are different sorts of lines and each line has a character of its own and can express a different mood, as the examples in Arabic from the Koran show on page 116.

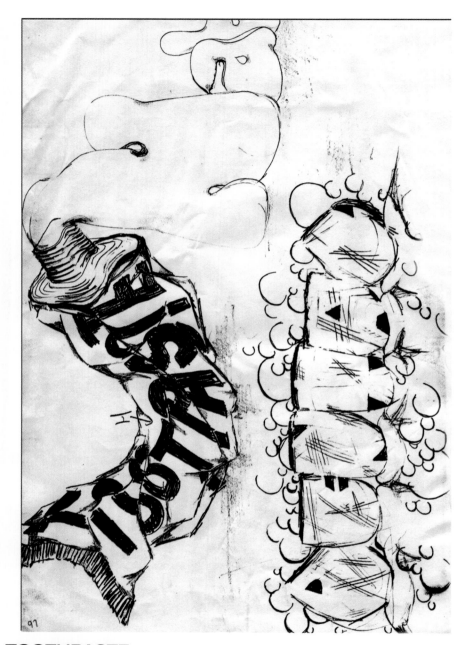

TOOTHPASTE.
Arabic influenced by a 15-year-old student.

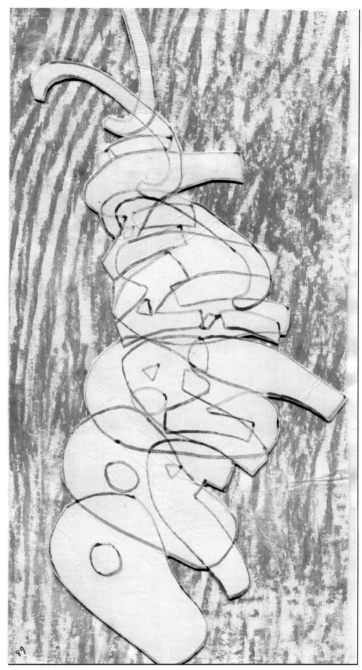

PANIC.
12-year-old –
pen and ink
on grained
rubbing –
feeling of fear
accentuated
by repeating
the word
through
action, moving
lines drawn to
express the
dog.

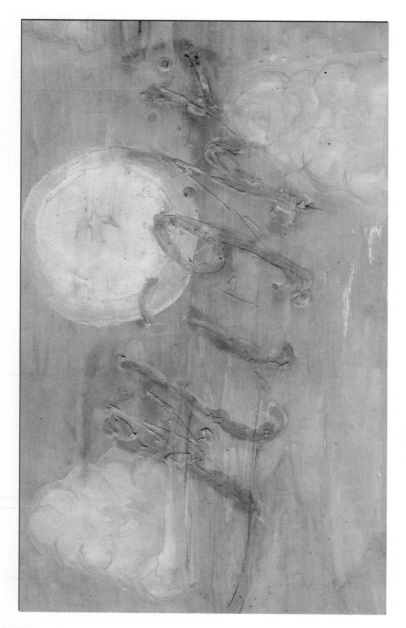

FLIGHT.
Flowing Arabic letters have inspired an 11-year-old student to create movement using wax and paint.

MOVING CURVES

ARMENIAN

Աա	ayb = A
Իի	eenee = e
Յյ	hee = H
Տտ	tyoon = D
Բբ	ben = P
Լլ	liyoon = L
Նն	noo = N
Րր	re = R
Գգ	geem = K
Խխ	khe = KH
Շշ	sha = SH
Ցց	tso = TZ
Դդ	da = T
Ծծ	tza = DZ
Ոո	vo = VO or O
Հհ	hyoon = W or U
Եե	yetch = YE
Կկ	ken = G
Չչ	cha = TCH
Փփ	pyoor = I
Զզ	zah = Z
Հհ	ho = H
Պպ	be = B
Քք	ke = K
Էէ	A = A
Ձձ	tsah = TS
Ջջ	ja = TSH
Ու	yev AND
Լլ	yet = E
Ղղ	ghat = GH
Ռռ	ra = R
Օօ	O = O
Թթ	to = T
Ճճ	djeh = J
Սս	sey = S
Ֆֆ	feh = For PH
Ժժ	jhay = S
Մմ	men = M
Վվ	vev = V

Շնորհավոր Նոր Տարի
Եւ
Ս. Ծնունդ

Happy New Year.

St. Gregory, Bishop of Armenia, converted King Tiridates III, making Armenia the first Christian kingdom as early as the fourth century A.D.

124

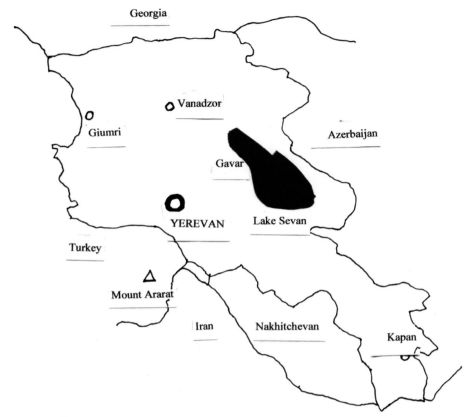

THE ARMENIAN ALPHABET

Armenia is a small but proud nation in the region of the Caucasus, between the Black Sea and the Caspian Sea.

It was the first nation in the world to adopt Christianity as its state religion. In fact, it celebrated 1,700 years of Christianity in the year 2001.

The Armenian Orthodox Church is an Apostolic Church, because the country was visited by two of the twelve Apostles – Thaddeus and Bartholomew.

THE ARMENIAN ALPHABET

Ա ա	Ff	Գ գ	Դ դ	Ե ե	Զ զ
ayb	ben	geem	da	yetch	za

Է է	Ը ը	Թ թ	Ժ ժ	Ի ի	Լ լ
eh	ut	to	jhe	ee-nee	yoon

Խ խ	Ծ ծ	Կ կ	Հ հ	Ձ ձ	Ղ ղ
khe	tza	ken	ho	dza	ghat

Ճ ճ	Մ մ	Յ յ	Ն ն	Շ շ	Ո ո
djeh	men	hee	noo	sha	vo

Չ չ	Պ պ	Ջ ջ	Ռ ռ	Ս ս	Վ վ
cha	be	ja	ra	se	vev

Տ տ	Ր ր	Ց ց	Ւ ւ	Փ փ	Ք ք
tycen	re	tso	hyoon	pyoor	ke

Ո o	Ֆ ֆ
o	feh

Հայր մեր որ յերկինս ես, սուրբ եղիցի անունն քո. եկեսցէ
արքայութիւն քո. եղիցին կամք քո, որպէս յերկինս եւ յերկրի: Զհաց
մեր հանապազորդ տո՛ւր մեզ այսօր. եւ թող մեզ զպարտիս մեր, որպէս
եւ մեք թողումք մերոց պարտապանաց. եւ մի՛ տանիր զմեզ ի
փորձութիւն. այլ փրկեա՛ ի չարէ:

[The Dominical Prayer]

**Our Father, who art in heaven, hallowed be thy name; thy
kingdom come; thy will be done on earth as it is in heaven. Give us this
day our daily bread; and forgive us our debts, as we forgive our
debtors; and lead us not into temptation; but deliver us from evil.**

A version of The Lord's Prayer in Armenian.

The Armenian alphabet consists of 38 letters, and was invented
in A.D. 405 by a professor called Mesrop Mashots. The alphabet
has been influenced by the Greek and Cyrillic alphabets because,
before he designed the Armenian letters, the people used Greek
letters for their written texts.

Acknowledged as one of the cradles of civilisation, Armenia is
justly renowned for its cultural heritage which includes churches
built in the early Christian basilica style of architecture, beautiful
manuscripts, distinctively woven carpets, and the establishment
of a university as early as the twelfth century.

Armenian alphabet – a Christmas card.

Our Father, who art in Heaven, hallowed by thy name; thy Kingdom come; thy will be done on earth as it is in heaven. Give us this day our daily bread; and forgive us our debts, as we forgive our debtors; and lead us not into temptation; but deliver us from evil.

A version of The Lord's Prayer in Armenian.

PROJECTS – PRACTICAL WORK

Ideas and suggestions for practical work

How the Armenian alphabet can be used by you:

- Armenian letters have a moving quality (walking sticks) about them which suits repetition.
- Sports – sporting figures distorted in movement.
- Serendipity – the faculty of making happy and unexpected discoveries by accident.
- Blob of ink – blow ink into Armenian letter-type figures.

Materials

The above can be carried out in a variety of media.

The examples shown will give you ideas as to what you can do.

"ԳԱԼՈՂ ԳԱՒԱԶԱՆԵՐ"

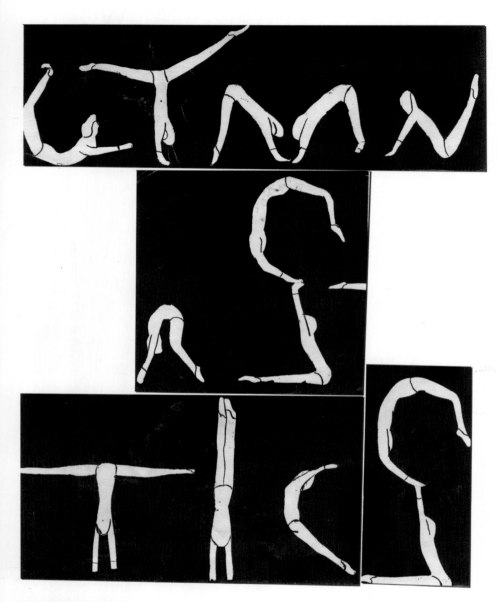

GYMNASTICS.

The moving curves of the human figure reflect both the Armenian alphabet and moving walking sticks. First draw the figures and then paint with black Indian ink.

130

GEORGIAN

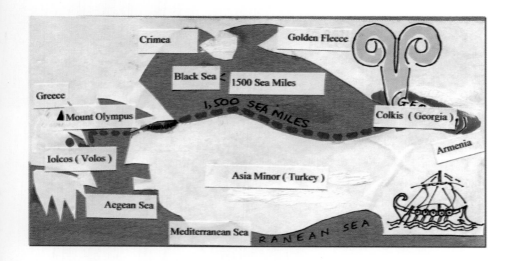

THE GEORGIAN ALPHABET

Georgia in ancient times was known as the Kingdom of Kholkis.

Jason and the Argonauts sailed in the galley – *Argo* – from central Greece across the Aegean Sea and into the Black Sea, a voyage of 1,500 miles. They hugged the coast of Asia Minor (Turkey) until they came to the fabled land of Chalkis (modern Georgia) in their quest for the "Golden Fleece". Sheep wading into the mountain streams trapped the flecks of gold in their fleeces creating a fable which has captivated the imagination of people for hundreds of years.

If true, Jason was Europe's first explorer.

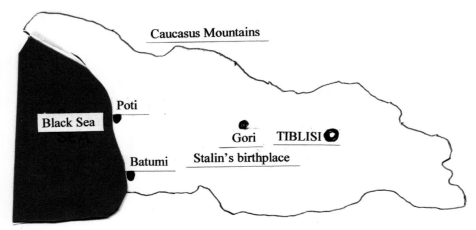

Georgians call themselves Kartvelebi and their country Sakarvelo.

The Georgian alphabet with 33 letters; some of the letters do not have an equivalent in the Roman alphabet.

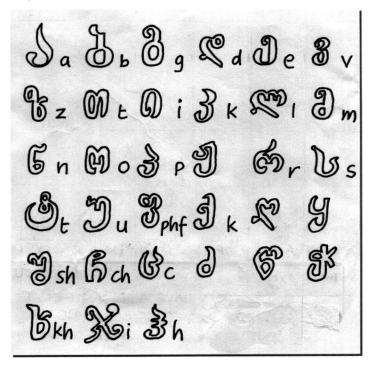

a	b	g	d	e
an	ban	gan	don	en
v,w,f	z	t	i	k
vin	zen	tan	in	kan
l	m	n	o	p
las	man	nar	hie	par
ž	r	s	t	u
zan	rae	san	tar	vie
phf	k	γ	q	sh
un	kan	gan	gar	sin
ch	c,ts	dʒ	ç	c̄
cin	can	jil	cil	tar
kh	i	h
xan	jan	hae

ამ ანბანში ახოთა რიცხვიდან ჩანს, რომ აღბანური
ენა ჩრდილო-აღმოსავლეთის კავკასიის ენების
მონათესავე ყოფილა.

ჩანს, რომ აღბანური ენა ახლანდელი უდური ენის
წინავარი ყოფილა.

გაამეორებინეთ ვიქცორს პროფებორის ნათქვამი! რომ
დავარაკმბდა, არ ვუხმენდი.

ნეხცორი ძილეებს ნელარ აკმევს! მე უკვე ვაჯამე.

ეხ ცნომა მიღებულ იქნა ვახცანგის გახცის შემდეგ.
თუმცა ქართული ენის ბრუნვათა რიცი ცრადიციითაა
დადგენილი, ეხ ბრუნვები თეორიულად შეიძლება
ხხვადახხვა რიცით იქნეს დალაგებული.

ანდაზა: უთქმელის მოქმელი თქმულმა შეჯახმთ.

ქართული ენის დამწერობაში წარმოუქმელი ახოები არ
არხებოსb.

ბახკური ენის მეუხწავლეელად ვერ გეცყვი, ქართული და
ბახკური ერომანეთს ენათესავება თუ არა.

ცხადია, კი, რომ ახეთი გენეციკური ნათესაობა ჯერ
ვიდევ დაუმცკიცებელია. ესე იგი, ეს გენეციკური
ნათესაობა აქამდის არ დამცკიცებულა.

ხამწუხაროდ, თანამედროვე ქართული ლიცერაცურული
ნაწარმოებების უმრავლეხობა ინგლისურ ენაზე ჯერ
ვიდევ გადათარგმნელია, ე.ი., ისინი ჯერ კიდევ არ
გადათარგმნილა.

ფელი უკვე ხმ არ გაგბავნილა? არ ვიცი; ვაყამ
ენდა გაგბავნოდა. მას კი თურმე არ მიუღია.
მეექქიცედეკ კათალიკონხა ოხცაც კონხცანცინე არხუკი-
მეს მცხეთის ხვეთიცხოვლის ცადარი აამენებინა.

ჩანს, რომ ამ ოხცაცნიხათვის მარჯვენა მოუჭრიათ.
დეცენცის მიხედვით, მეფე გიორგი ჰირველმა თავის
ჯალათ არხუკიძიხათვის მარჯვენა მოაჭრევინა.

ეხ თურმე იმიცომ მომხდარა, რომ მეფე გიორგის
მეუყვარებულმა, მმცენერმა შორენამ, მეფეს
კონხცანცინე არხუკიძი ამჯობინა.

The Georgian alphabet is possibly derived from a variety of eastern Aramaic alphabets, although Georgian underwent some changes due to Greek influence, with the advent of Christianity in the country.

PROJECTS – PRACTICAL WORK

Ideas and suggestions for practical work
How the Georgian alphabet can be used by you:
- Georgian letters have a human figure-like quality which allows the person to be distorted in many ways.
- Role play – make words do what they are saying.
- Illustration – design some humorous figures such as clowns or nursery rhyme characters to put around the room in a playgroup.
- Surgery – design some figures in a medical context to put around the walls in a doctor's waiting room.

Materials
The above can be carried out in a variety of media.

The examples shown will give you ideas as to what you can do.

DANCE.
12-year-old – movement and dance – paint on paper with a symbolic figure in action through repetition.

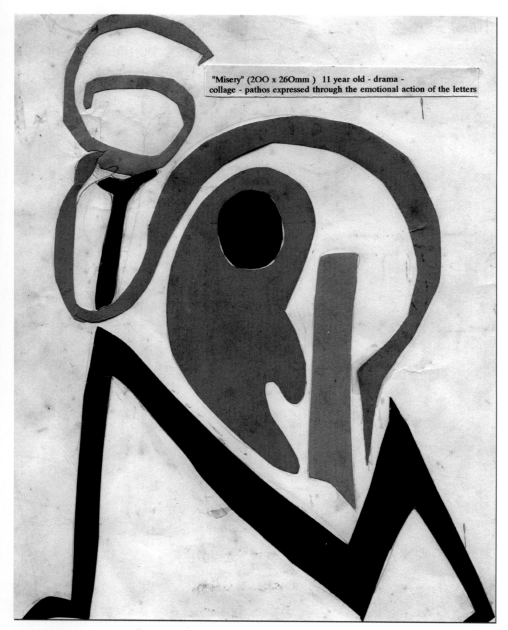

"Misery" (2OO x 26Omm) 11 year old - drama - collage - pathos expressed through the emotional action of the letters

MISERY.

11-year-old – drama collage – pathos expressed through the emotional action of the letters.

138

BOUNCE.

11-year-old – movement and dance – plastic on paper. The bright
red, yellow and blue echo the delight of such a toy as the Jack-in-
the-box.

ST. KEVIN OF IRELAND.

celtic

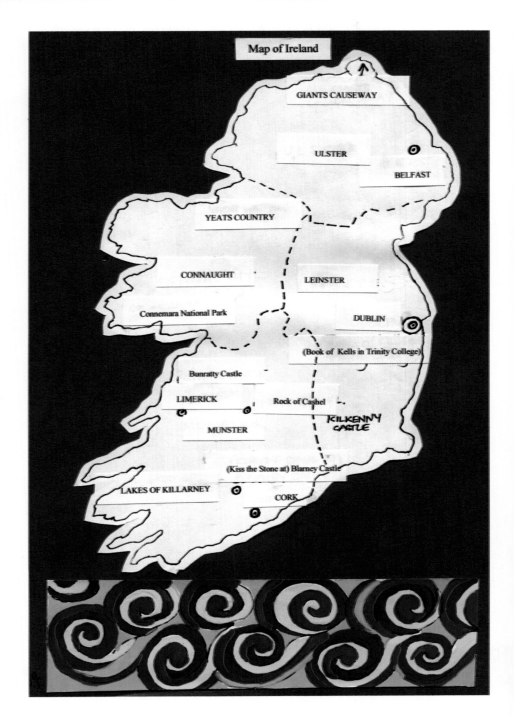

Map of Ireland

GIANTS CAUSEWAY

ULSTER

BELFAST

YEATS COUNTRY

CONNAUGHT

LEINSTER

Connemara National Park

DUBLIN

(Book of Kells in Trinity College)

Bunratty Castle

LIMERICK

Rock of Cashel

KILKENNY CASTLE

MUNSTER

(Kiss the Stone at) Blarney Castle

LAKES OF KILLARNEY

CORK

THE CELTIC ALPHABET

Between the sixth and ninth centuries in Western Europe, and particularly in Ireland, monks and scribes designed letters, patterns and decorations which were truly exquisite. These beautiful letters appeared in the Book of Kells, the Book of Durrow, and that of Lindisfarne in about 800 A.D.

Christianity is expressed in these illustrated Gospels, which were the works of writers who were dedicated to the beauty of creation. Indeed, the Books of Kells and Durrow are some of the finest artwork known, and they have inspired everyone since their creation. The Book of Kells is to be found in Trinity College, Dublin, while the Book of Durrow is in The British Museum in London.

As well as in famous books, the Celtic alphabet was used to decorate objects such as weapons, armour, cups, and crosses. Motifs for decoration were taken from many sources such as plants, flowers, animals, birds, as well as the human form, often as saints. These motifs were transformed into abstract ornamental, geometrical designs, often incorporating spirals and sweeping curves. Human figures, where they do appear, are always depicted in an abstract manner.

The written text used in books at this time was Gaelic. Gaelic is one of the two main branches of the Celtic languages, and involves Irish Gaelic, Scottish Gaelic, and Manx (Isle of Man).

Ireland was a Gaelic-speaking nation until the sixteenth century when English became rather more important. Today, Ireland has become officially bilingual and Irish Gaelic is now a core subject in primary and secondary schools.

Ireland has produced four great Nobel Prize winners in G. B. Shaw; W. B. Yeats, S. Beckett and Seamus Heaney, as well as writers such as Jonathan Swift, Oliver Goldsmith, Richard Sheridan, Maria Edgeworth, Sean O'Casey, Brendan Behan and James Joyce.

Gaelic words which are now part of the English language include: bard, glen, bog, slogan (a short, catchy phrase used in advertising) whiskey, shamrock, brogue, and galore.

Ireland's Celtic Heritage.

The Irish have a great tradition of storytelling, and Irish folklore is rich in tales of fairies, leprechauns, banshees, and other supernatural beings. Fairies lived under mounds of earth, leprechauns were the "little people", while banshees were female spirits.

St Patrick, whose name day is the 17th March, is the national saint of Ireland. The shamrock is worn on his day in parades and pilgrimages.

Celtic Letters

Celtic letters were often drawn using a pen of broad or narrow nib width, in brown or black ink. They were outlined in red dots giving the effect of a tint. The eye mixes the red dots and white spaces, perceiving pink as the result. Dots were used to give a spiritual impression of floating across the page. The negative spaces inside the letters were coloured yellow. Alternately, letters were outlined and inked-in using a fine brush.

In the Book of Kells, letters appear as decorated black shapes in themselves or as animals.

Letters also appear as AMPERSANDS, i.e. a compound of two letters e.g. "ET" from the Latin meaning "and" "&".

PROJECTS – PRACTICAL WORK

Ideas and suggestions for practical work

How Celtic letters can be used by you:

- Celtic letters are particularly expressive.
- Role play – make words do what they are saying.
- Lino cutting – design your initials and print on paper or material. Remember to reverse and cut your design on the lino block.
- Initials – design personal letter paper and put your monogram on it.
- Illustration – design a book cover, or music programme, or play information cover.

Materials

The above can be carried out in a variety of media including lino blocks, tools, inks and materials as well as printing papers.

The examples shown will give you ideas as to what you can do.

SLIME.
Mixed media work by a 13-year-old student. Draw the outline of the letters, taking care to make the word do what it is saying. A mixture of wax, ink, and paint is effective here.

MAD.

The word does the action – the action is the word in this piece by a 14-year-old student. A collage using cellophane, tissue paper and silver paper.

STRETCH.

The word does the action – the action does the word in this piece by a 13-year-old student. Expressive letters cut in plastic.

CYRILLIC
ALPHABET

ВАРИАТИОНС
ОН А ТХЕМЕ
"VARIATIONS ON A
THEME"
РУССКИЙ
АЛФАВИТ

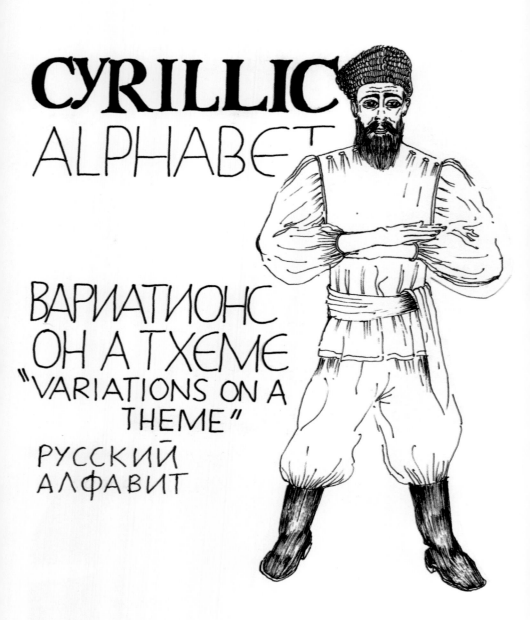

Lands that use the Cyrillic alphabet.
Armenia and Georgia have their own alphabets.

The type of pattern to be found on an iconostasis in a Russian Orthodox Church.

THE CYRILLIC ALPHABET

Аа	Бб	Вв	Гг	Дд
a	be	ve	ge	de
Ее	Жж	Зз	Ии	Йй
e	zhe	ze	ee	kratkoe
Кк	Лл	Мм	Нн	Оо
ka	el	em	en	o
Пп	Рр	Сс	Тт	Уу
pe	er	ess	te	oo
Фф	Хх	Цц	Чч	Шш
ef	kha	tse	che	sha
Щщ	Ъъ	Ыы	Ьь	Ээ
shcha	trerdiyznak	yeri	myagkiyznak	e
Юю	Яя	Ёё		
yu	ya	yo		

ANOTHER VERSION OF
THE CYRILLIC ALPHABET

А А a	Б в b	В v v	Г g g
Д D d	Е YE e, ye	Ж ZH zh	З Z z
И I i	Й Y ĭ, i	К K k	Л L l
М M m	Н N n	О O o	П P p
Р R r	С S s	Т T t	У U u
Ф F f	Х KH kh, x	Ц TS ts, c	Ч CH ch, č
Ш SH sh, š	Щ SHCH shch, šč	Ъ no sound	Ы I ï
Ь no sound	Э E e	Ю YU yu, ju	Я YA ya, ja
Ё YO yo			

THE CYRILLIC ALPHABET

The Cyrillic alphabet, with different modifications, is used in Russia, Ukraine, Belorussia, Serbia and Bulgaria. Although these languages are Slavonic, it is important to remember that the Slavonic languages of Eastern Europe include also Polish, Czech, Slovakian, Croatian, Slovenian and Macedonian.

The Slav people who are Orthodox in religion use the Cyrillic alphabet, whilst those practising the Roman Catholic faith use the Roman alphabet.

The Cyrillic alphabet is named after St Cyril, who with his brother Methodius are known as the Apostles of the Slavs. They were, in fact, Greeks from Thessaloniki in Northern Greece, and it is they who adapted the curved Greek alphabet of the ninth century which provided the model on which the modern Cyrillic alphabet is based. They also translated the scriptures and the Orthodox liturgy into Slavonic.

The alphabet as used in Russia consists of 33 letters, greatly resembles Greek (many letters are exactly the same), and is always written from left to right.

The Russian alphabet can roughly be divided into four groups of letters:

- Those that look and sound like English letters – А Т О М К
- Letters which look like English letters but sound different – С Р Е В Н У Х
- Letters which are different but with similar sounds – П Л И З Д Ф Ю Г Б Й Ё Я
- Letters unlike English letters – Ж Ц Ч Ш Щ Ы Ь Ъ

Moscow = М О С К В А
Saint Petersburg = С А Н К Т–П Е Т Е Р Б У Р Г

Святитель Николай Чудотворец. Икона нач. XVI в. Новгород

Saint Nicholas the "Miracle Worker" 16th Century icon, Novgorod, Russia.

153

An ICON is a picture, usually of a saint, of a church feast, of the Virgin Mary, or of Christ.

It is to be found in an Orthodox Church and is there to be used by the worshippers. Icons are a way of telling people about some part of Christ's teaching in a simple, straightforward way.

In visual terms, an icon must be seen as a window. It is usually on a board or on wood and the figure of the saint appears flat. Shapes and colours are often very bright and can look strange, precisely because the painter is showing his idea of heaven.

There is not so much concern with 3-D form and very little technical interest in perspective.

Colours are also symbolic. The gold background signifies heaven; the Virgin Mary usually appears in blue; while Christ wears brown or dark-blue robes.

Most icons have some letters in Greek or Russian to explain what the icon is all about. The letters are an integral part of the whole design and words are often painted vertically as well as horizontally. Capital letters dominate, but smaller, lower-case letters are used, and are sometimes interspersed between the capitals.

И осподобитися намъ слы-
шанію святаго Евангелія, Господа Бога молимъ. Премудро-
сть, прости, услышимъ святаго Евангеліа. Миръ всѣмъ.

Отъ Іоанна святаго Еван-
геліа чтеніе. Вонмемъ

Сущу позпѣ въ день той
во едину отъ субботъ, и две-
ремъ затворенпымъ идѣже
бяху учеппцы Его собрани,
страха ради Іудейска ; прии-
де Іисусъ и ста посредѣ и
глагола имъ : миръ вамъ.

И сіе рекъ, показа имъ
руцѣ и нозѣ и ребра своя;
возрадовашася убо учеппыци,
видѣвше Господа.

Рече же имъ Іисусъ паки :

миръ вамъ ; якоже посла Мя
Отецъ, и Азъ посылаю вы.

И сіе рекъ, дуну, и гла-
гола имъ : пріимите Духъ
Святъ. Имже отпустите грѣ-
хи, отпустятся имъ, и имже
держите, держатся.

Ѳома же единъ отъ обо-
юнадесяте, глаголемый бли-
зпецъ, пе бѣ ту съ ними,
егда пріиде Іисусъ.

Глаголаху же ему друзіи
ученпцы : видѣхомъ Господа.
Онъ же рече имъ : яще пе
вижу на руку Его язвы гвоздппныя, и вложу перста
моего въ язвы гвоздппныя,
и вложу руку мою въ ребра
Его, не иму вѣры.

An example of Cyrillic letters from the Gospel according to St John,
(Chapter 20, verses 19–25) written in 'Old Church Slavonic'.

Russian Letters Used as an Integral Part of Communist Poster Design

The poster has always been a powerful means of communication. To be effective, a poster should be simple in design with a minimum of subject content; include a message which is to the point and in colour, and that is eye-catching so as to have maximum impact. It should transmit its message instantly, and leave an indelible imprint on the mind long after the observer has ceased to have the poster in front of him.

Under the Communists in Russia, for most of the twentieth century, the poster was a particularly important means of communication as propaganda. Loyalty to the collective state, the need to spread Marxist ideas to a largely illiterate population, to extol the virtues of hard work both in the countryside and in the factory, made the poster an essential means of getting the Communist message across.

Posters encouraging people to support the revolutionary cause were produced in their thousands by the Soviet regime.

The hammer and sickle were, with the red star, the symbols of the Union of Soviet Socialist Republics and appeared on the Russian flag between 1917 and the collapse of the communist system in 1991.

Russia
By slizerone
http://slizerone.deviantart.com/art/Russia-53422841

CONSTRUCTIVISM was a twentieth century Russian art movement, aimed at creating images for post-revolutionary New Russia. Artists such as Vladimir Tatlin, Olga Rosanova, Alexander Rodchenko and Varvara Stepanova, as well as Naum Gabo, created works in sculpture, painting, stage design, posters, slogans, architecture, furniture, and typography.

This group felt that art should fulfil a social role and that artists should be "artist engineers". They were initially influenced by Cubism and Futurism but, unfortunately, a lot of Russian Constructivist works were destroyed through official Communist disapproval of abstract art.

Cyrillic letters have had some influence on abstract painting.

Wassily Kandinsky, born in Russia in 1866 and who died in 1944, was the first abstract painter in modern art.

Essentially, there is no subject matter as such in his paintings as he wanted "to create a work of art so as to create a world". He eliminated all representational elements from his art and expressed his emotions through the power of colour.

However, by 1923, Kandinsky was painting in a more geometrical manner based on squares, circles, triangles, and lines; all essential components of Cyrillic letters.

Author's word inspired by Russian letters. WOMAN has been used
to create the top of the coffee table design; made of clay tiles on

which angular-type letters complement the shape of the table.

PROJECTS – PRACTICAL WORK

Ideas and suggestions for practical work
- How the Russian alphabet can be used by you.
- Posters – Russian letters look particularly dynamic when giving a message.
- Icons – design your own icon and include your initials.
- Easter Eggs – paint and decorate your eggs with personal messages.

Materials
A variety of media can be used including eggs and seasoned wood if you are going to paint an icon. You will also need gold paint.

The examples shown will give you ideas as to what to do.

Why not pay a visit to a large airport and observe the airlines from Eastern Europe from the spectators' viewing area. You will see Cyrillic letters on the side of each aircraft, including:

Russian Airlines: А Э Р О Ф Л О Т

Yugoslav Airlines: Ј А Т. Ј У Г О С Л О В Е Н С К И А Э Р О Т Р А Н С П О Р Т

Balkan Bulgarian Airlines: В А Л К А Н

Other countries use the Cyrillic alphabet on their national airlines – how many others can you see?

EASTER is the most important celebration in the Orthodox Church calendar. The Resurrection of Christ occurs after forty days of fasting, His crucifixion and burial, and the triumph of life after three days of death.

Eggs are symbolic of Easter for Orthodox Christians. They are dyed red, symbolising the blood Christ shed to save mankind from its sins, and are often decorated in different patterns or with messages using letters.

Decorate Eggs – letter messages on eggs

- First boil the eggs for about half an hour or until hard.
- Add the dye, made preferably from edible food colours – beetroot, apple skins, coffee, spinach, and dandelion leaves make the best colours.
- Allow the eggs to go cold before drawing your pattern of letters on them using wax crayons.
- Scratch the design on with a knife.
- Melt candle wax and drip your pattern of letters over the egg. When it hardens, dip the egg into the dye again to get a lighter version of letter pattern.
- Paint your letters on, using acrylic paint or poster paint.
- When the letters are dry, varnish your eggs using olive oil, applying it with cotton wool.
- All sorts of personal messages can be communicated, but none more appropriate than:

ХРИСТОС ВОСКРЕС

JAPANESE

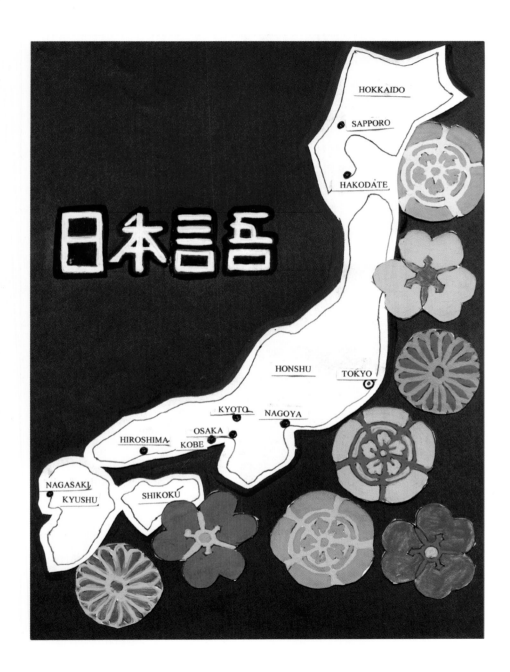

日本語

HOKKAIDO

SAPPORO

HAKODATE

HONSHU   TOKYO

KYOTO   NAGOYA

OSAKA

HIROSHIMA   KOBE

NAGASAKI

KYUSHU   SHIKOKU

THE JAPANESE ALPHABET

The Japanese language is Nihongo

Japan 日本

Japanese 日本語

日本 "Suns" describes Japan as the place east of China where the sun rises. This is where the term "Land of the Rising Sun" comes from.

a	ka	sa	ta	na	ha	ma	ya	ra	wa
あ	か	さ	た	な	は	ま	や	ら	わ
ア	カ	サ	タ	ナ	ハ	マ	ヤ	ラ	ワ

i	ki	shi	chi	ni	hi	mi		ri	
い	き	し	ち	に	ひ	み		り	
イ	キ	ツ	チ	ニ	ヒ	ミ		リ	

u	ku	su	tsu	nu	fu	mu	yu	ru	
う	く	す	つ	ぬ	ふ	む	ゆ	る	
ウ	ク	ス	ツ	ヌ	フ	ム	ユ	ル	

e	kesu	se	te	ne	he	me		re	
え	け	せ	て	ね	へ	め		れ	
エ	ケ	セ	テ	ネ	ヘ	メ		レ	

o	ko	so	to	no	ho	mo	yo	ro	(w)o	n
お	こ	そ	と	の	ほ	も	よ	ろ	を	ん
オ	コ	ソ	ト	ノ	ホ	モ	ヨ	ロ	ヲ	ン

The Japanese took various Kanji and simplified them to produce two syllabaries: Hiragana (which are round, easy-to-use characters, or Kana) and Katakana (which means practical, because the script is based on straight simplified lines).

JAPANESE – 46 characters (letters)

The Japanese alphabet of 46 characters is a mixture of letters derived originally from Chinese and Korean. It is a very different language in structure, even so. An educated Japanese knows around 2,000–3,000 characters (Kanji) while more educated scholars know around 5,000 Kanji.

Japanese can be written horizontally from left to right, or more traditionally in vertical columns from right to left. Books, newspapers, magazines, and official documents are usually written in vertical lines.

Japanese is written without spaces between the words. Children in school tend to write horizontally and the letters they use are forms they see in graphics rather than characters learned in calligraphy.

Calligraphy in Japan is known as SHODO, and was introduced to Japan along with Chinese writing in the seventh century A.D. Calligraphy has always been considered an essential accomplishment for the cultured person. Brush and ink are the traditional tools used.

The Japanese writing system can be classified as follows:

- Kanji – Chinese character.
- Kana – Phonic alphabets.
- Hiragana – round, easy-to-use characters.
- Katakana – means practical.

The Japanese call their country Nihon or Nippon.

Japanese art has always been associated with the wonderful craft-form called woodblock printing. Indeed, in the eighteenth and nineteenth centuries Japanese porcelain was exported to the west wrapped in beautiful woodblock-printed wrapping paper.

Geisha
By *j-alex-darr

PROJECTS – PRACTICAL WORK

Ideas and suggestions for practical work
How Japanese characters can be used by you:

- Comic/Manga – design your own comic or college rag.
- School/ College Magazine – including Japanese pictograms in your illustrations.
- Lino Cutting/ Woodblocks – Japanese characters are particularly suited to lino cutting and woodblock printing. Enjoy cutting into the material. Don't forget to reverse the design so that the print comes out the right way.
- Poster – a dramatic subject with punchy impact so as to drive the message home.

Materials
A variety of materials can be used including lino and woodblocks. Print on beautiful handmade Japanese papers.

The examples shown will give you ideas as to what to do.

MANGA – COMICS
The illustrated comics produced in Japan on a weekly/monthly basis are known as Manga, which is the Japanese for comics. The sheer diversity of literature produced is extraordinary and has a massive following among young people.

Manga is instantly recognisable. The subject matter is usually centred on an adolescent who finds himself in a number of situations and circumstances which he endeavours to overcome. The presentation is one of instant impact due to the fusion of picture, punchy Japanese letters expressed mostly in black and white, and accentuated by two bright colours.

One reason Manga is popular with young people is that it is a form of escapism. Japanese are conditioned from an early age to show particular respect for people in authority. Manga allows the young individuals to escape from daily formalities to a new-found freedom.

Japanese-
inspired
fashion "graffiti".
Japanese-type
characters printed on
cotton, chiffon, silk and
towelling.

Manga
By lenouszka

Japanese woman
By RedMantis

Japanese characters have always been used as an integral part of a Japanese print whatever the subject.

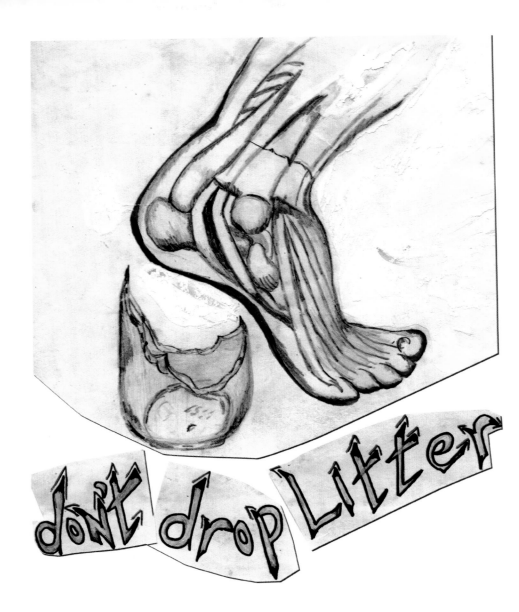

DON'T DROP LITTER.
The spiky, jagged letters echo the linear angular characters of Japanese letters in their simplest form. By a 15-year-old student using pencil and biro.

LETTERS

as black and white pattern

Gothic
or Blackletter

MUSICIAN AFTER ALBRGCHT DÜRER 1503/04

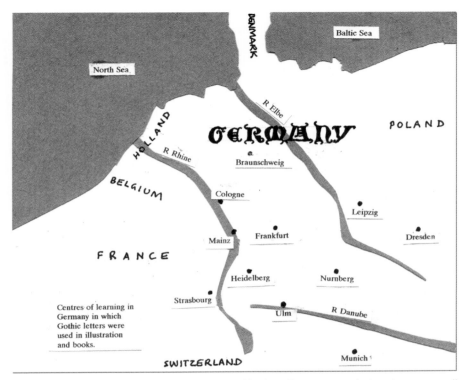

Centres of learning in Germany in which Gothic letters were used in illustration and books.

Johannes Gutenberg (c. 1400–1468), the German printer, is generally considered the inventor of printing from movable types. He lived and worked in Mainz and Strasbourg.

Until movable letters held together by a frame were invented, letters were cut on a wood block. Books combined printed letters with illustrations. The technique of printing letters and pictures, called a woodcut, was a particularly popular art form with the Expressionists in Germany around 1910.

GOTHIC LETTERS

Gothic letters evolved in northern Europe from the middle of the twelfth century. In many ways these letters are similar to the fundamental forms associated with architecture, i.e. the pointed arch prevailed. They appear close and narrow, and angular with generally acute corners and pointed tops.

Gothic letters are often called 'Blackletters'. The term Blackletter should strictly be applied only to letters in which the amount of black in the line overbalances the white. Usually, the less white space the better, for its beauty depends on an overall unity of positive black and white pattern.

Beautiful initials designed by Durer. 16th Century.

176

Albrecht Durer, 1471–1528

Albrecht Durer is one of the great artists of the High Renaissance. He was a prolific painter and engraver who also wrote copiously on architecture and sculpture. He lived and worked most of his life in Nurnberg, a great cultural and commercial centre at the crossroads of Europe.

Although he established his reputation in religious works, exquisitely observed detailed drawings, and painting of animals, he regarded the human body and its proportions, and letters as the central concern of his art. However, it is in the field of calligraphy, of which he was a pioneer, that he is particularly admired.

Blackletters designed by Durer. 16th Century.

"Ist euch nicht Kristus erschienen?"
"Did not Christ appear to you?"
Woodcut by Karl Schmidt-Rottluff.)

This poster for "The Bridge" (Die Brucke) Exhibition in 1909 by Max Pechstein includes the portraits of fellow artists Ernst Kirchner, Eric Heckel, Karl Schmidt-Rottluff and Max Pechstein himself. The stark, almost caricature, depiction of the faces makes a striking image of positive/negative and recalls the Gothic approach to letters and the play between black and white spaces.

EXPRESSIONISM 1905–1920

Expressionism is a term applied to a style of painting, sculpture, graphic art, and literary work which is concerned with the inner world of feeling.

It is Germany's most significant contribution to twentieth century art.

The movement is not so concerned with imitating nature, but rather distorts natural appearance in order to convey what the artist feels about something.

Woodcut by Ernst Ludwig Kirchner.

Blaue Reiter front cover of catalogue by Wassily Kandinsky.

Expressionism centred on two groups of artists, namely Die Brucke (The Bridge) in Dresden, and Blaue Reiter (The Blue Rider) in Munich.

Franz Mon
Abstraktion

ABSTRAKTION 1963 by Franz Mon.
A play of black and white – Op, or Optical, Art is based on the
idea that the designer can create optical effects that persuade the
spectator to see the visual illusions.

PROJECTS – PRACTICAL WORK

Ideas and suggestions for practical work
How Gothic letters can be used by you:

- Gothic letters and designs are best carried out in black and white, where impact is achieved through bold contrast.
- Pen Work – draw the letters in black ink.
- Wallpaper – positive and negative subject matter in black and white.
- Wrapping Paper – geometric shapes based on letters.
- Woodblock or Lino – remember to cut letters back to front if they are to print in the correct sequence and direction.

Materials
A variety of black and white, especially paints, inks and papers. Also woodblocks and tools.

The examples shown will give you ideas as to what you can do.

Gothic letters using a pen. The sequence of strokes and pen direction are indicated above.

Design for wallpaper.
"O" by a 12-year-old student. A collage of black and white, counter-change. Although these shapes are not angular, the balance between positive/negative space recalls the Gothic concern with equal balance.

Gothic letters make an
eye-catching heading.

Wrapping paper.
"H is for Horse" by a 14-year-old student using black and white
paint.

MUSIC by 16-year-old student.
Paintwork inspired by the Expressionists. The linear content of the features and hair takes on the role of musical notes based on the Blackletter type.

Different types of S – symmetry in letters.

Each of these S examples is made up of bars which are the same thickness and are equally balanced. A play of red, black, and white in alternate design, each S is a square letter of symmetry. By a 15-year-old student.

LETTERS as DECORATED SYMBOLS

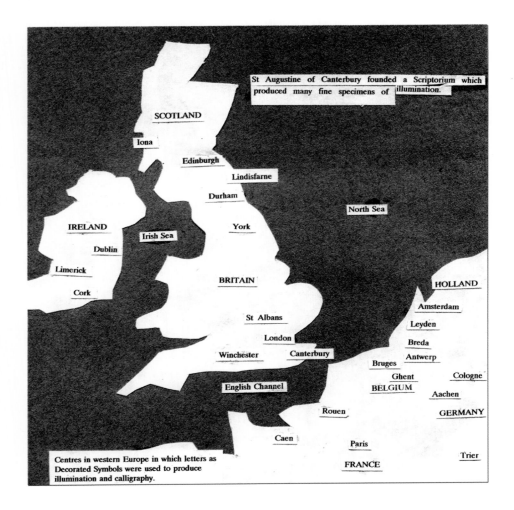

St Augustine of Canterbury founded a Scriptorium which produced many fine specimens of illumination.

SCOTLAND

Iona

Edinburgh

Lindisfarne

Durham

North Sea

IRELAND

Irish Sea

York

Dublin

Limerick

BRITAIN

HOLLAND

Cork

Amsterdam

Leyden

St Albans

Breda

London

Antwerp

Winchester

Canterbury

Bruges

Ghent

Cologne

English Channel

BELGIUM

Aachen

Rouen

GERMANY

Caen

Paris

Trier

Centres in western Europe in which letters as Decorated Symbols were used to produce illumination and calligraphy.

FRANCE

Letters as Decorated Symbols

Decorating letters has a long and noble pedigree, stretching back to Roman documents, Celtic Ireland in the sixth to ninth centuries, and through to the present day.

The purpose of illumination in Christian Bibles and other religious texts in the past was to glorify and embellish the Word of God. As such, illumination has constituted an important artistic feature of human expression.

In Western Europe, Christian monks carried out illumination and calligraphy. These artists excelled in using everything and anything as ornament. In Ireland, Britain, France, Holland, Belgium, and Germany, ornamentation as a form of illustration was depicted using flowers or fruit, interspersed with animals, birds, and human figures, often eccentrically conceived. They embellished and accentuated capital letters which were heightened with gold, sometimes flat, and occasionally brilliantly burnished.

Heraldry – a form of illustration which often includes letters

Heraldry is a personal "trademark". In the past, particularly in the Middle Ages, each man wore a distinctive display of "arms". These became personal symbols and were an important means of identification because few people could read in those days.

Arms were usually depicted on a shield. The shield, and other display liveries such as helmets, crests, mottos etc; are known collectively as "the achievement".

HAMLET
PRINCE OF
DENMARI

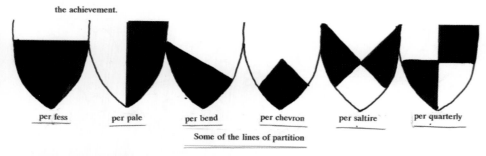

per fess | per pale | per bend | per chevron | per saltire | per quarterly

Some of the lines of partition

The shield was partitioned into recognised divisions, emblazoned with letters and mottos, often in Latin, as well as the cadency marks (the position of a person in their family). In addition, as with illumination, animals, birds, or stylised flowers completed the design.

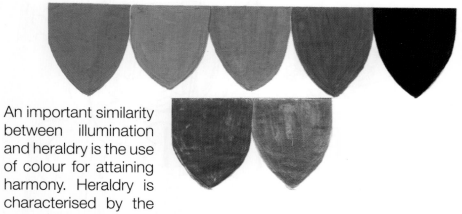

An important similarity between illumination and heraldry is the use of colour for attaining harmony. Heraldry is characterised by the use of five tinctures: red/gules, blue/azure, black/sable, purple/purpure, green/vert and two metals gold/or and silver/argent, which replace yellow and white. The use of metallic colours, especially gold and rich hues, are essential components of illuminated letters.

Eldest son | second | third | fourth | fifth | sixth | seventh | eighth | ninth

Cadency marks are very small heraldic charges usually placed in the upper/centre part of the shield.

192

Your Arms and You

You can have a lot of fun designing your own arms. Get your family to take part and make it a collective effort.

You might even want to submit your effort to the College of Arms in London to be officially recorded if it is approved.

When designing a shield, personal information such as parental origin, place of birth and personal interests can be included.

PROJECTS – PRACTICAL WORK

Ideas and suggestions for practical work

How Illumination-type letters can be used by you:

- Illuminated letters lend themselves to so many design projects, but especially to:
- Book Illustration – for headings, covers, and titles.
- Heraldry – design your own coat of arms or a design for your college, school, society, or company.
- Initials – design your own monogram.

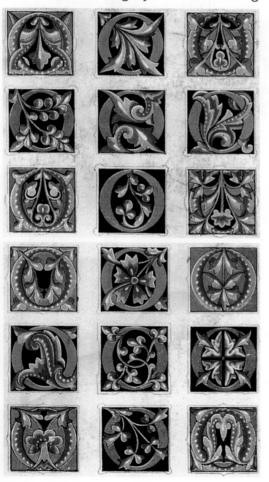

Materials

A variety of media can be used including gold and silver paint, poster paints, brushes and other tools.

The examples shown will give you ideas as to what you can do.

THE VERSATILE S.
Illumination – painted
Linear dot and stroke pattern – felt-tip pen
Hissing snake – blackline
Gravestone – rubbing.

Have fun designing your own MONOGRAM based on your INITIALS.

Use a felt-tip italic pen to draw a dot and stroke pattern.

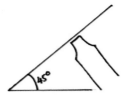

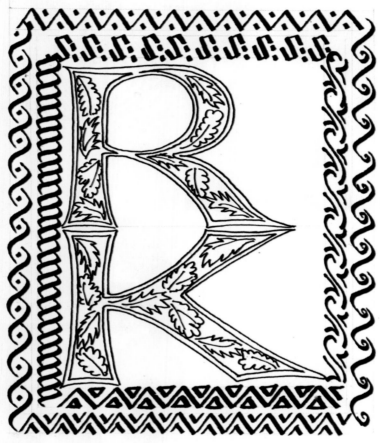

Decorated symbol letters for your initials

- Draw your initials one above the other.
- Remember to leave space around the letters for the dot and stroke pattern.
- Hold your italic pen or felt-tip pen at an angle of 45 degrees. The nib remains in this position throughout the design.
- Add colour to the letters if you wish.

Large original letter by a 13-year-old boy in paint.

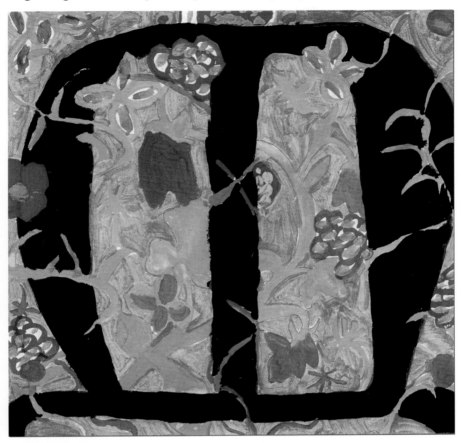

Your Illuminated Capital Letter

To design your illuminated capital letter, begin by using good quality paper. The letter looks particularly good when drawn in a square.

Draw the letter first with a pencil. Add the flowers, stems, leaves, and any other subject matter fairly carefully. You will want to add details in colour as you go along. Paint your main areas of colour first, leaving the gold until last. A restricted colour scheme is best, i.e. the red family with green, blue with orange.

PROJECTS – PRACTICAL WORK

Ideas and suggestions for practical work

How this type of letter can be designed by you:

- Draw up the word you wish to use in simple block capital letters.
- Try to get the bars that make up each letter the same width.
- Join up all corners to the same vanishing point.

Materials
Use colours and media of your choice.

 The examples shown will give you ideas as to what you can do.

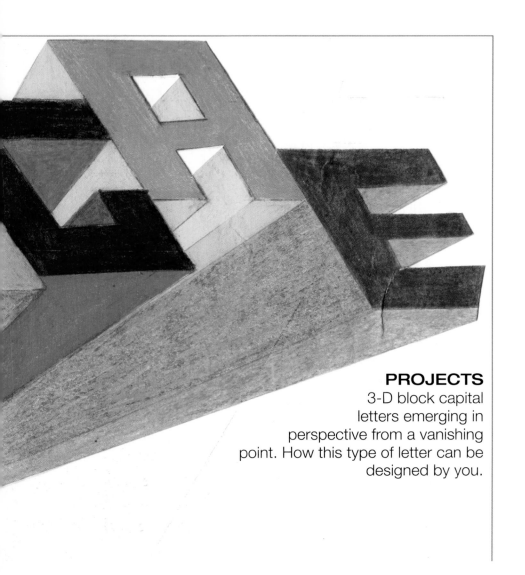

PROJECTS
3-D block capital letters emerging in perspective from a vanishing point. How this type of letter can be designed by you.

Large original letter of the twelfth century.

eXplore SECTION TWO

DESIGN VALUES AND VISUAL APPRECIATION EXERCISES

Now that you are aware of different letters and alphabets, you will realise that some of the design elements in them are to be found also in geometric shapes, symbols, road signs, proportions of the human figure and buildings, and even in the variety and silhouettes of trees.

It can be great fun looking for and finding similarities between the letter forms of different alphabets and these other means of communication.

Look at the following exercises and work through them. By undertaking the exercises, it will help sharpen up your visual appreciation of letter forms and what goes to constitute letters in an alphabet.

A lot of the subject matter from the practical work has been incorporated where possible. All the illustrations are based on the design values of CONTRAST, EDGE, ISOLATION, OVERLAP, POSITION, PROPORTION, RHYTHM, READABILITY, and SPACE, and were drawn or selected in black and white to further clarity of perception.

In addition, each design value has an appropriate piece of practical work of art in colour.

CONTRAST –	Black and white communication – (progression).
	Black/red/white – (geometric design).
EDGE –	Electric E (warm colours).
	Face "horror" (features).
ISOLATION –	A for apple (transformation).
OVERLAP –	Woman as a guitar (etching).
	Eurodress in black and gold (fashion).
	Red/brown letters (overlapping capitals).
POSITION –	15 EU maps (countries in national colours).
	"Hello" (mouth to ear).
PROPORTION –	Christ (in majesty).
RHYTHM –	Melt (wax).
	Spring (tiger).
READABILITY –	Brochure (design using tissue paper).
	Wallpaper (collage design).
SPACE –	Hanging Italy (a letter L).
	Hiccup (collage).

DESIGN VALUES AND LETTER FORMS

CONTRAST, EDGE, ISOLATION, OVERLAP, POSITION, PROPORTION, RHYTHM, READABILITY, SPACE

Most people are familiar with at least one alphabet as a means of communicating with others. The design values usually associated with letter forms correspond to their use in other subject areas also.

CONTRAST

Contrast helps the discerning eye distinguish one shape, colour, or subject from another and this is especially so for national flags, as in letter types. Colour opposites such as black/white, red/green, blue/orange, purple/yellow make for contrast.

EDGE

Edge means that the outline of a letter, symbol, or object can stand out clearly from its surroundings. This is important in fabric design, lino cutting and tile motifs as well as in alphabets. Serifs, the ends of vertical, horizontal or diagonal strokes, give Roman letters a clean edge and a "proper" finish.

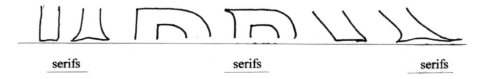

serifs   serifs   serifs

ISOLATION

When emphasis is required or attention needs to be focused in poster design, informative road signs or the façade of a building, isolation is all-important. The isolated letter or object has impact and stands out.

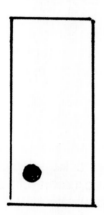 

OVERLAP

Can be another way of giving the illusion of depth on a flat surface. Tonal shading and diminishing scale is not always appropriate in needlework, wallpaper design or fabric printing, so overlap is an alternative means of giving "punch". "Bubble Writing", where the letters overlap each other, is highly favoured by children.

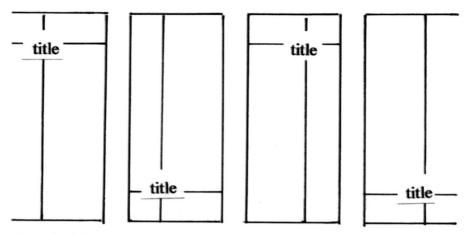

POSITION

The position of a letter, word, or slogan on a page, book cover, or poster, as well as the position of a symbol for a town on a map, is a necessary requirement in these practical forms of communication. Position helps to encourage understanding.

you can read this
you cannot read
this very well

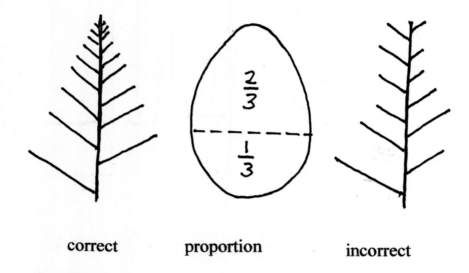

$\frac{2}{3}$

$\frac{1}{3}$

correct   proportion   incorrect

PROPORTION

A design value of very real importance in nature. Proportion maintains a pleasing balance.

In nature, proportion can be found in:
- the measurements of the human body.
- the spiral of a snail shell.
- the distances between rows of branches on a fir tree which taper to the top.
- the overall measurements of an egg.

This proportion in natural and man-made things is often referred to as the GOLDEN MEAN or GOLDEN SECTION, and was known and used by the ancient Greeks through their use of mathematics.

"If a thing is divided into two parts, the smaller is in the correct scale or size to the larger part, as the larger part is to the whole."

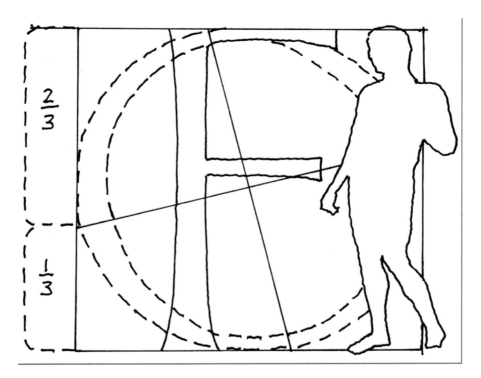

In the human figure, the head is the right size to the body, as the body is to the total height of the person. To the ancient Greeks, in the perfectly proportioned man, the head fitted into the total height of the man 7 or 7 1/2 times.

An egg can be divided into two parts. The smaller part is correct in scale to the larger part, as the larger is to the overall size of the egg.

To draw a capital F based on this principle:
- First draw a square.
- Divide the two vertical lines on either side of the square into two parts.
- Draw a diagonal line between the two.
- Draw the capital O. Remember the Roman O was constructed at an angle. Remember also to put the "thins" and the "thicks" in the appropriate positions.
- The F can then be drawn in the appropriate place in relation to the O.

RHYTHM

When letters appear on a page, rhythm is the natural flow of the words across it, and these words can enhance the visual presentation of the page. So as to be pleasing to the eye, and to give words, sentences and layout a coherent unity, rhythm is the overall effect of the whole display.

There are some aesthetic details worth considering. Some offer an alternative way of recording details. Others focus the eye and the brain on an important point or position where emphasis is required.

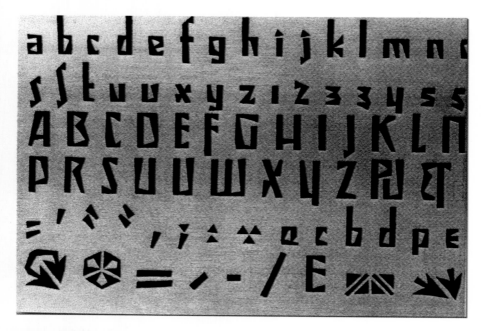

READABILITY

The all-essential requirement, if a letter or an alphabet is to be used appropriately and informatively. Readability is fundamental to understanding what is being said.

Letters, when cut up and re-arranged, can be used to produce new visual ideas. As these pieces are built upon each other, new and unexpected relationships result that have simplicity and graphic vitality.

BRAZIL

SPACE

Without space – that is, the play of positive and negative shapes which characterise letters – alphabets are rendered almost meaningless.

Use of letters in the Czech Republic.

In this alphabet design by Vojtech Preissig, 1916, the empty negative spaces in each letter help to form the essential character of the alphabet.

A contemporary sculpture made up of letters in space, in the Czech capital of Prague. The letters are from different alphabets of fellow European Union countries.

PROJECTS

At the end of each alphabet section in this book, there are project suggestions and ideas which can be carried out in your practical work. Here are some ways you might want to consider when you are carrying out your own work.

1. The EMOTIVE CONTENT of letters – "Emotive Letters".
2. The DEVELOPING and STRUCTURING of letter forms – "The Logos".
3. Words that take on the VISUAL APPEARANCE of their meaning – "Letters in Action".
4. Letter forms which allow a choice to be made between ALTERNATIVES – "Positive and Negative Relationships".

Below are a few examples selected from the Alphabets and the Design Values and Appreciation Exercises incorporating the four areas.

- EMOTIVE LETTERS e.g. Hebrew "faces"; Celtic "mad"; Japanese "don't drop litter".
- THE LOGOS e.g. Chinese "brochure"; Hebrew "typeface"; Roman capital O, C, and A; Arabic "buzz off"; Russian "woman"; Illumination "reggae" and "your arms and you".
- LETTERS IN ACTION e.g. Hieroglyphics "tired" and "old"; Arabic "panic" and "flight"; Georgian "bounce" and "misery"; Gothic "music"; Celtic "slime" and "stretch".
- POSITIVE AND NEGATIVE RELATIONSHIPS e.g. Sanskrit "grace"; Greek "Doric" and "palindrome"; Armenian "gymnastics"; Gothic "H for horse".

In addition, to help you consider alternative possibilities when using letter forms and alphabets in design, the following questionnaires have been devised which might help you with your ideas. If you like designing letters or words with an EMOTIVE content, consider the eight questions in questionnaire 1. Which of the eight is the most important to you?

1. Questionnaire 2 has six questions based on developing and structuring the LOGOS. This area puts particular emphasis on the content and what is being communicated.
2. Letters and words with instant impact and ACTION are to be found in questionnaire 3 and you will enjoy the freedom to express the meaning and visual appearance of your subject matter when designing.
3. Pattern work in all its varied forms is surely a favourite in art, and the seven questions in POSITIVE and NEGATIVE RELATIONSHIPS will help you with your endeavours.

CONTRAST

" Communications " (2OO x 23Omm) steady progression through different letter types - black ink on white.

CONTRAST has been achieved here using:
  1. Black and white.
  2. Fine and solid letter forms.

- Divide your paper into ten equally spaced lines.
- Draw up the different letter types, taking care to use a variety of styles.
- Complete using black ink or paint.

Optical weight and thickness.

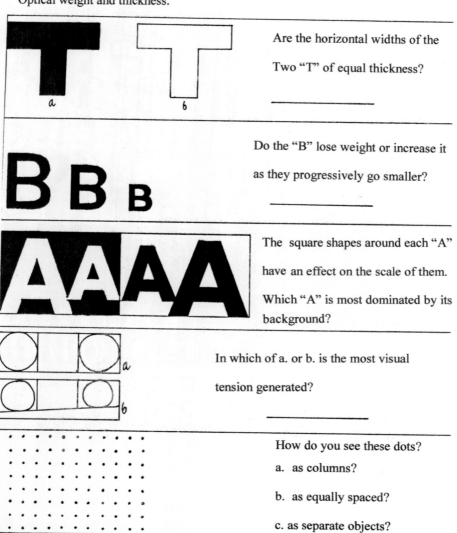

Are the horizontal widths of the Two "T" of equal thickness?

_____

Do the "B" lose weight or increase it as they progressively go smaller?

_____

The square shapes around each "A" have an effect on the scale of them. Which "A" is most dominated by its background?

In which of a. or b. is the most visual tension generated?

_____

How do you see these dots?

a. as columns?

b. as equally spaced?

c. as separate objects?

A design based on a simple capital T, using the stark contrast of sharp colours like red, black, and white.

- Interlock the basic letter shape into four directions, north/south/west/east.
- Draw up your design in pencil based on equally spaced vertical and horizontal lines.
- Paint the interlocking pattern in red, black, and white.

5-letter "A" line, shape, pattern, texture, tone.

For each letter "A", write the appropriate description.

Line. shape. pattern. texture. tone.

EDGE

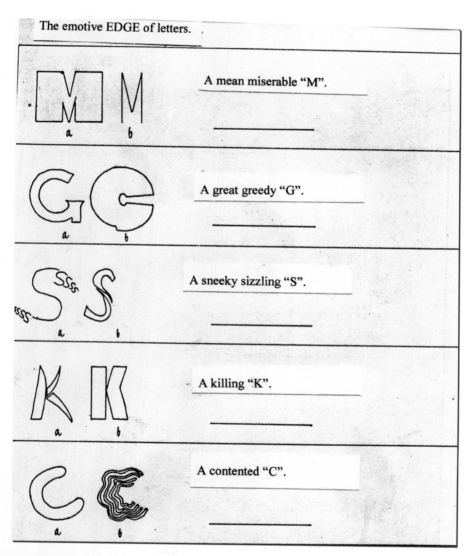

A mean miserable "M".

A great greedy "G".

A sneeky sizzling "S".

A killing "K".

A contented "C".

An Electric E

Red, orange and yellow are warm colours and help to put over heat.

Draw up your letter. Think about the emotional impact of shape and colour. Paint using appropriate family of colour.

Other examples: a fat F, a musical M, a killing K, a big B.

"Horror"

The word can be an amalgam of letters that are drawn up and painted, or are cut out of newspapers and magazines.

For an eye-catching impact, include features such as a mouth, an eye, or the profile.

ISOLATION

A PALINDROME, as stated earlier, is a word or statement that reads identically backwards and forwards.

little level letter	_____
dog gag sag	_____
poop coop loop	_____
banana anna magna	_____
defer confer refer	_____

Pick the five palindromes from the list of words above.

ISOLATION is the perception of an object aided by the clarity and isolation of the image.

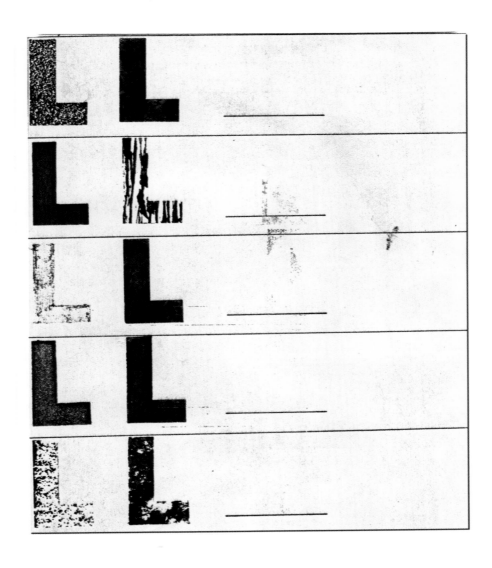

For each pair of letter Ls, write the appropriate quality:
 Textured/mottled, matt/shiny, light/dark, fuzzy/sharp, smooth/rough.

Often, perception of an object is hindered by an inability to see the whole of a recognisable form.

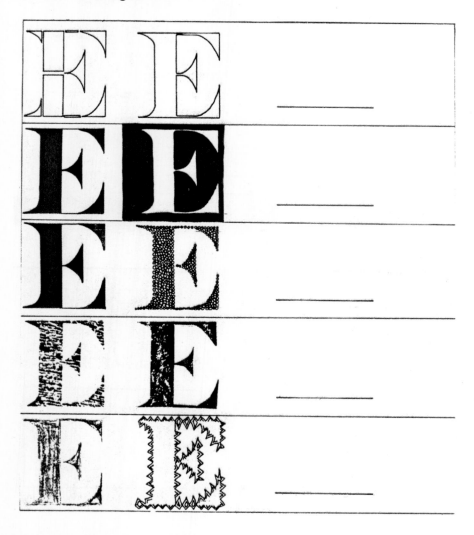

For each pair of Es, write the appropriate quality:
    Flat to electric, solid to dots, positive to negative, hard to soft, units to whole.

"Transformation" letters lend themselves to being changed. In this example, a letter goes through various isolated stages of development to becoming an apple. Two colours are used in reverse order from stage one to stage six. Impact is assured through complementary colour.

OVERLAP

"Woman"

These two projects use "Woman" as their subject. All the design elements are juxtaposed to form a collage.

Cut out the subject matter from various sources. Consider composition carefully by placing pieces in different positions. Only stick the pieces down when a satisfactory arrangement has been achieved.

"The Euro Dress"
The theme here is to design an evening dress suitable for an international occasion. Black/white/gold makes for a dramatic effect.

Which letter has been used here?

_____

What do you see in the word shadow?

a. merely shadows of the letters?

b. raised letters casting shadows

SHADOW

Which is the odd letter in this row?

CDG M OS

_____

Only the counter shapes in the pattern

of each letter have been used here.

What is the word?

_____

The critical parts of a letter.

Which 4 letters appear here?

_____

By overlapping lower case and capital letters using two colours, a lively pattern has been created.

POSITION

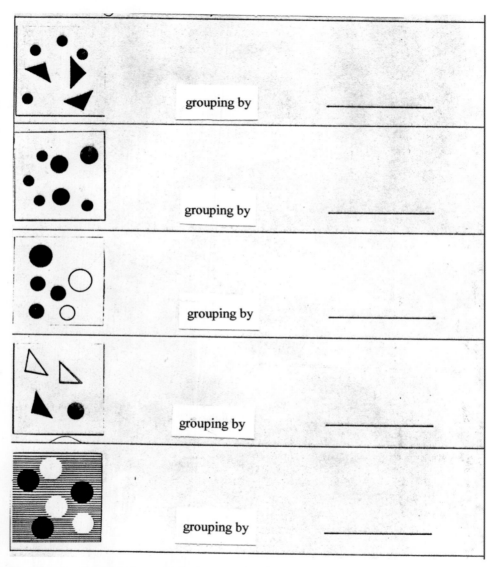

grouping by _____

grouping by _____

grouping by _____

grouping by _____

grouping by _____

Circles and triangles - circles and triangles are basic shapes in letters.
Beside the appropriate grouping place: shape, tone, size, shape and tone, size and tone.

THE EUROPEAN UNION

Each country has been carried out in a type of letter association with its national character.

- BRITAIN: *"Letters"* is drawn in a solid, sensible block capital which clearly echoes a national trait.
- GERMANY: *"Buchstaben"* exhibits the Gothic type with its vitality and energetic lines.
- BELGIUM & LUXEMBOURG: *"Lettre"* a modern version of the Art Nouveau style.
- SWEDEN: *"Bokstäver"* an open type of letter which expresses the progressive country.
- ITALY: *"Lettere"* a modern version of the Roman capital letter, the basis for most western alphabets.
- GREECE: *"Grammata* (Γράμμάτά)*"* an angular type of letter reminiscent of its own ancient alphabet.
- HOLLAND: *"Letters"* flaunts a direct type of letter which is in keeping with its international outlook.
- FINLAND: *"Kirjaimet"* is associated with its flair for modern design.
- SPAIN: *"Cartas"* displays the flamboyant exuberance of the Moorish style.
- AUSTRIA: *"Buchstaben"* evokes letters with a musical disposition.
- FRANCE: *"Lettres"* appears in the Art Nouveau style.
- DENMARK: *"Bogstaver"* presents its clean-cut image.
- PORTUGAL: *"Letras"* recalls its nostalgic past.
- IRELAND: *"Letters"* displays its charming Celtic tradition.

A map of fifteen of the twenty-seven countries that make up the European Union and Switzerland. Each country is depicted using a letter type which describes the national character, and a colour which appears in its national flag. The word for LETTERS is in each country's own language. Each of the word groupings appears in the correct position in relation to the map of Europe.

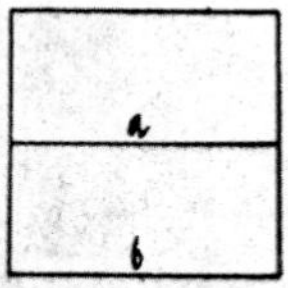

The square is divided into 2 equal parts.

Which part looks smaller? _____

_____

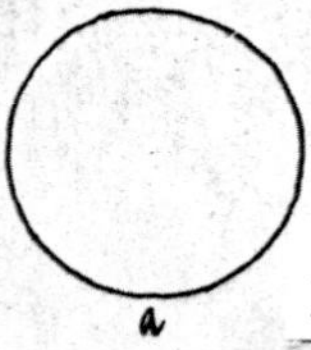

Is the same as?

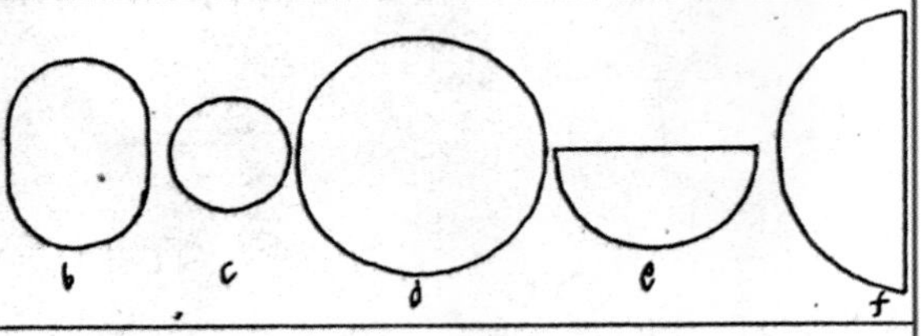

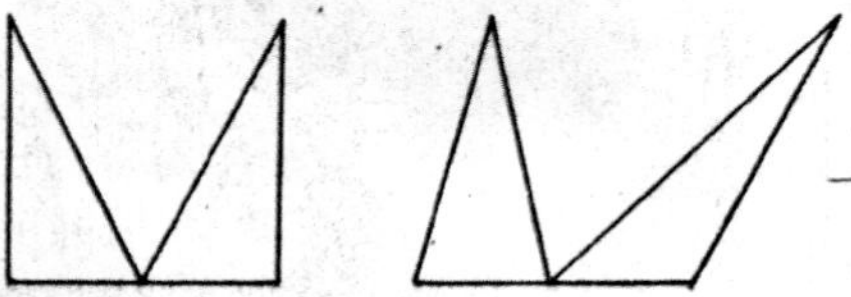

Are the 2 solid areas of the letter "M" equal?

_____

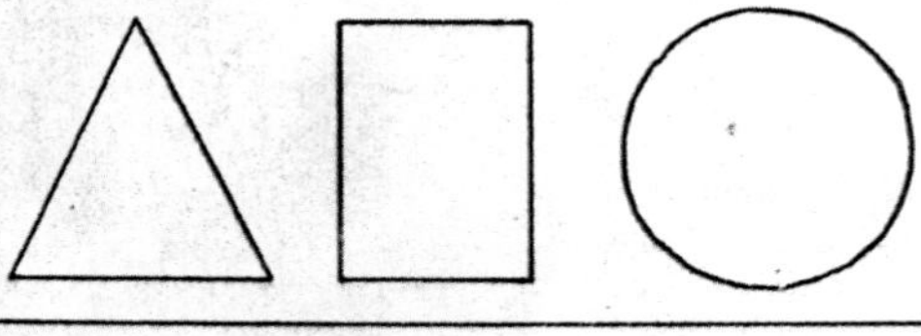

Are these three solid figures the same width?

_____

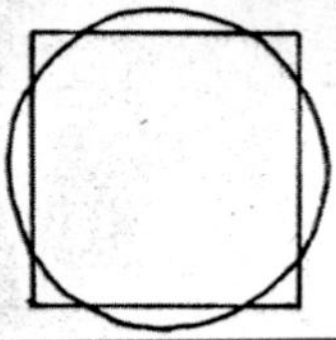

Are the circle and the square of equal area?

_____

_____

231

HELLO.
Work by a 12-year-old girl – drawing using pen and black ink.

PROPORTION

"Christ"

The letters are on either side of the head and as part of the halo. The shape and symbolism of the hand composing the letters with the fingers are in proportion to the overall size of the icon.

Letters as used in Byzantine art depicting an icon of Christ, in Majesty.

Letters have always formed an integral part of an icon. Here, Christ's right hand is composed in the blessing. The index finger is vertical and the second finger slightly bent, making the letters I C, the first and last letters for the Greek word for Jesus. The thumb is stretched out and the third finger is bent, making the letter X. The little finger is slightly bent, making the letter C.

X and C are the first and last letters of the Greek word for Christ.

The simple diagrams of trees echo the proportions of five capital letters.

For each of the tree shapes, write the appropriate capital letter: A E I M V.

ABCDEFGHIJ
KLMNOPQR
STUVWXYZ _____

ABCDEFGHIJKL
MNOPQRSTUV
WXYZ _____

ABCDEFGHIJ
KLMNOP2R
STUVWXYZ _____

AABCDEFGHIJK
LMNOPQRST
UVWXYZ _____

ABCDEFGHIJ
KLMNOPQRS
TUVWXYZ _____

Letter typefaces as used in printing.

For each of the letter typefaces, write the appropriate name:
Countdown, Brush Script, Ringlet, Old English, Times New Roman.

RHYTHM

"Melt"

- Draw up and action word.
- Melt wax and fill in the letters.
- Cover the wax with coloured inks.
- Contrast the background in complementary colour.

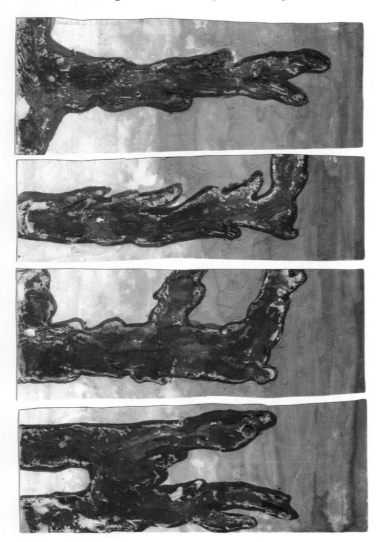

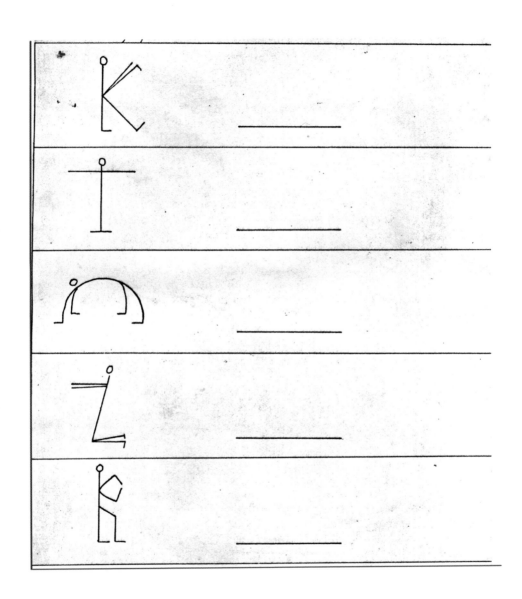

_____

_____

_____

_____

_____

Letter Role Performance
For each of the enacted letters, write the appropriate capital letter.

"Tiger Springing"

With onomatopoeia, letter shapes take on the visual appearance of their meaning.

- Draw an animal in line, preferably in action.
- Fit the letters into the outline.
- Adjust the shape of the letters to carry out the action.

Letter Role Performance.

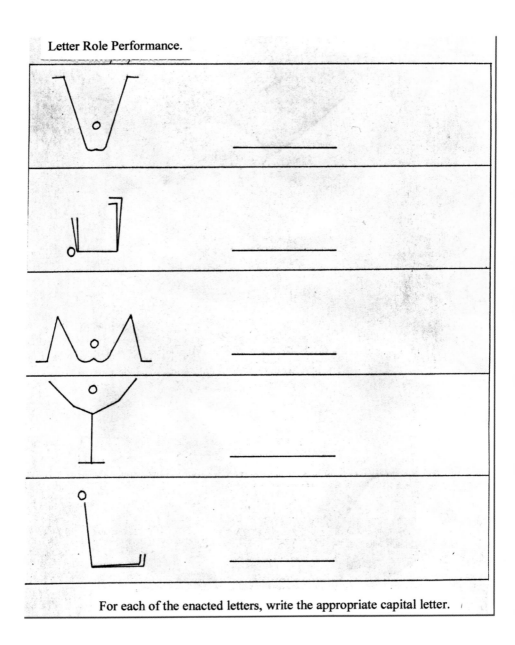

_____

_____

_____

_____

_____

For each of the enacted letters, write the appropriate capital letter.

READABILITY

"Brochure"

A brochure is information which can be easily carried.

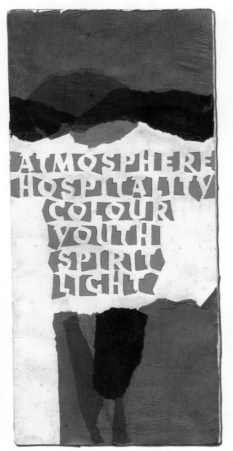

- Divide up a sheet of card into four equal parts (making eight sides).
- Each side should have an illustration and information.
- The overall "feel" i.e. subject matter, colour, layout, and design, should give the brochure unity.
- Above all, the brochure should convey its contents through immediate readability and eye-catching impact.

Squares, circles, and rectangles underlie the forms of capital letters which make for readability.

The hallmark of Greece, her landscapes, her buildings the scenes she evokes, is the way she inspires us with unique individuality.

In his Antigone, Sophocles' theme is:
"many marvels there are, but none so marvelous as man".
Hospitality is a Greek's form by nature.

Greece is youth, the vitality of its inhabitants. The Home of Democracy, of justice and human dignity.

When in Greece you become essentially a creature of light and spirit, believing that the lucidity of the mind can put an end to the darkness of the soul.

Believing in Spirit, you cannot escape the fact that you are a sharer and partaker of divine radiance.

Greece is bathed in light unlike any other light on the surface of the Earth. It is a light that can be tasted and drunk.

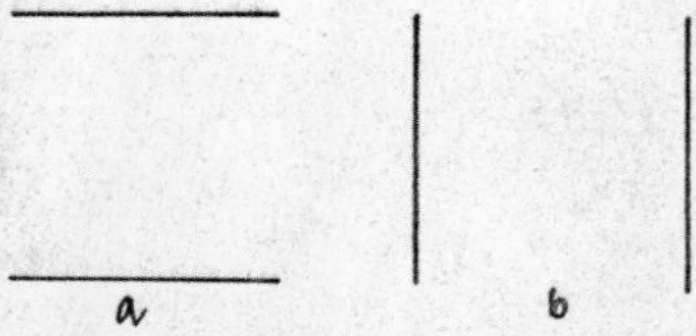

Lines at sides of 2 squares.

Which square looks wider?

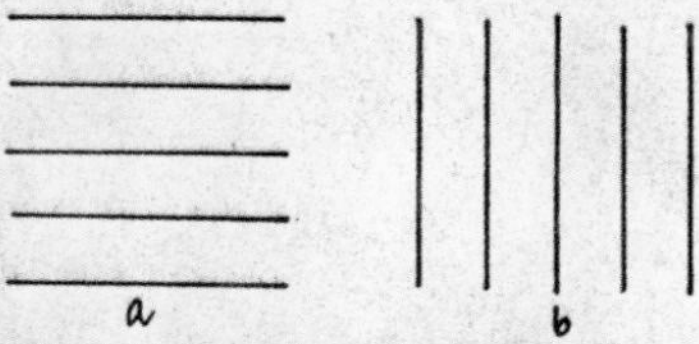

_____

Squares filled with lines.

Which square looks taller?

_____

2 small black and white squares.

Which square appears smaller,

the black surrounded by white

or the white by black?

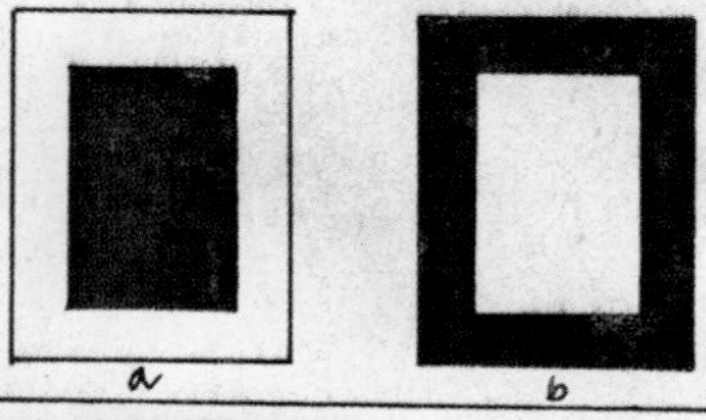

Black and white rectangles.

Which rectangle looks larger?

_____

A grey circle on a black and a
white rectangle. On which
rectangle does the grey circle
look lighter?

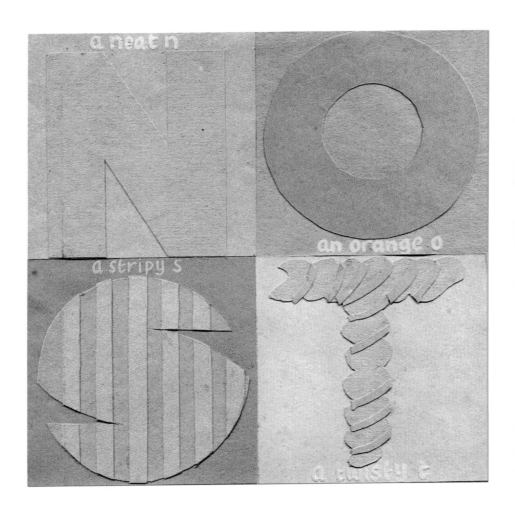

a neat n

an orange o

a stripy S

a twisty t

"Wallpaper"

Wallpapers help to create a mood for a room. They should enhance the atmosphere without dominating it. In this design for a child's bedroom, the letters encourage the child to read the alphabet and to associate the letters with relevant subject matter. The gentle, subtle colours give the room a restful atmosphere.

f☐rst

☐dd

div☐de

☐tract

☐ultiply

1 − ✖ ➗ ✚

For each of the above words, write the appropriate symbol in the box in each word.

SPACE

When we look at unfamiliar alphabets, our eyes are forced to view, initially, the pattern and textural quality.

Идя навстречу требованиям жизни и по желаниям наших читателей, мы изменяем ся, расширяемся и совершенствуемся.

Стремясь решить труднейшую задачу удовлетворения запросов самых разно образных категорий читателей, мы осве щаем широкий круг вопросов: печатное дело, оформление, история, археология философия, поэзия и даже занятейшные приключенческие рассказы из жизни контрабандистов. Когда мы оглядываемся назад, то мы ищем вдохновения для будущего! Когда мы глядим вперед, то мы надеемся помочь наиппание за номеризацию печати

لقد توسّعنا وتغيّرنا ونأمل أن نكون أفضل. في عام غفير الأفراح واجهنا مشكلة أن لكن صرفية لسانا رغم مقابلة إرضاء إن لم يكن إدخال السرور على طبقات كبيرة من القراء في شتى الموضوعات: فلسفة وتاريخ، نكاية وفنون. قصص تمسي بلهفة. ولا نهال تطبيق العلم والمرح في عصرنا هذا، ولقد استوحينا من ما في ماضينا، وعند ما ننظر الى هذا المستقبل نؤمن بهذا الجميع القادم والماضين معنا رقم إحداثهم سيكونون صورة صغيرة لنا عنده الجنسيات بكل هذا. أنا نو أن نتحدث مع قرائنا كل بلغة ومكان نقدم بأكبر عدد من الفئات على قدر ما يسمح الكان، وإننا لننظر في بناء بقدر إرادتنا.

For each of the five languages, write the appropriate name:
Arabic, Hindi, Hebrew, Greek, Russian.

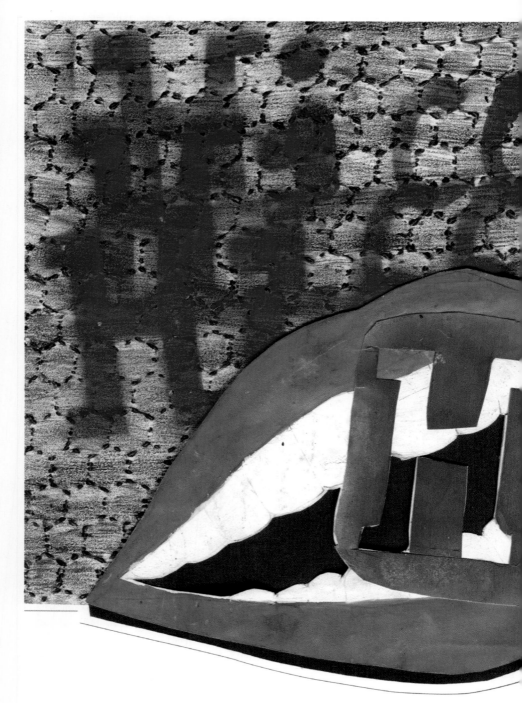

"Hiccup"

A feeling of 3-D is created here because the tongue hangs out from the mouth which itself stands out from the background. Repetition of the word "Hiccup" creates the stress and embarrassment associated with this action. The background is a rubbing from chicken wire with the word "Hiccup" sprayed on using an aerosol can, while the tongue has letters cut out with a Stanley knife.

"Italy"

Making the familiar strange and the strange familiar. Here, Italy is seen as a letter L.

Seen in its recognisable position in Europe, it is a leg or boot shape, but it can also be seen as a letter T or J.

We certainly do not expect to see Italy hanging from the sky in SPACE.

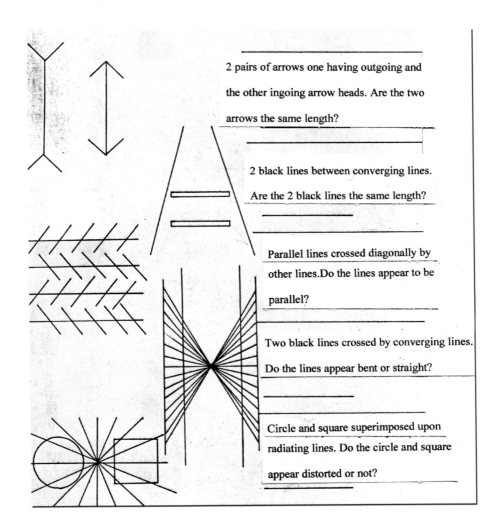

2 pairs of arrows one having outgoing and the other ingoing arrow heads. Are the two arrows the same length?

2 black lines between converging lines. Are the 2 black lines the same length?

Parallel lines crossed diagonally by other lines. Do the lines appear to be parallel?

Two black lines crossed by converging lines. Do the lines appear bent or straight?

Circle and square superimposed upon radiating lines. Do the circle and square appear distorted or not?

SECTION THREE

FOUR QUESTIONNAIRES

"Emotive", "Logos", "Letters in action", "Positive and Negative Relationships"

"Enjoy Using Letters" is a ten-week programme of study using letters and alphabets as a basis for personal expression.

The project and practical work in this book should be an encouraging stimulus for this course.

QUESTIONNAIRE ONE –
Emotive Letters

1. Which emotion have you chosen (e.g. contented, sad, happy, depressed, miserable, surprised, angry, frightened)?
2. What type of letters have you chosen to express your emotion?
3. Which came first, the letter type or the subject matter?
4. Was the subject easy to put down on paper?
5. Have you spent enough time on developing the idea?
6. Are you pleased with the way the letters form part of the overall design?
7. Does the design and what the word is saying convey its meaning instantly?
8. Which of the design elements (line, colour, pattern, shape, form) have you used the most?

I think question... is the most important because...

QUESTIONNAIRE TWO –
The Logos – Developing and Structuring of Letter Forms

Put the list of six below in order of personal importance.

1. Letters are simple shapes in themselves.
2. Letters are based on geometric shapes – circles, squares, triangles.
3. Letters and words are fun because you can do so much with them.
4. Letters are "definite things" so it is easier to "start off" in art.
5. Letters make art as a subject closer to other subjects.
6. Letters have design patterns that are easy to adapt into whatever you like.

I think question... is the most important question because...

QUESTIONNAIRE THREE –
Letters in Action

1. Does the word you have been using take on the appearance of its meaning?
2. Is there a lot of movement in your design?
3. By using a word in this way, has it helped you to have a deeper understanding of it?
4. Does the design and what it is saying convey instant meaning?
5. Which of the design elements (line, colour, pattern, texture, shape, form) have you used most?
6. Which was the most difficult part of the design to do?

I think question... is the most important question because...

QUESTIONNAIRE FOUR – Positive and Negative Relationships

1. Has black and white made it easier to see the outline of your design?
2. Have you used the shapes and spaces around, inside and between each letter equally as for the letters themselves?
3. What is it about black and white that helps you design your letters?
4. Does the meaning stand out clearly?
5. Is black and white easier to use than colour?
6. Which of the design elements (line, colour, pattern, texture, shape, form) have you used the most?

I think question... is the most important question because...

A TEN WEEK COURSE OF LESSONS USING LETTERS

ENJOY USING LETTERS IN ALL THEIR FORMS

Work Topic Studied

1. Talk of alphabets: Hebrew Greek, Roman, Celtic etc.

2. Roman alphabet proportion, layout, spacing, entasis.

3. A Roman capital O.

4. The illuminated medieval letter.

5. Monograms

6. Italic writing – week 1.

7. Italic writing – week 2.

8. Mobiles and decorations.

9. Words and pictures.

10. Personal study.

A TEN WEEK COURSE OF LESSONS USING LETTERS

ENJOY USING LETTERS IN ALL THEIR FORMS

Practical Session

1. Historical perspective: how letters and alphabets developed – possible connections between them – their use by artists.

2. Carry out the basic essential of letters in a practical "hands on" way.

3. O the basic letter on which all the letters are designed using measurement, carried out in different materials: paint, collage etc.

4. Personal initials using gold and silver – "Coat of Arms".

5. Designing initials in modern type.

6. How to do Italic writing. Letters make patterns – make words.

7. Using it creatively – greeting cards, letter headings etc.

8. 3-D letters, hanging and free-standing letter forms.

9. Making the word do what it is saying – action words.
   Take one of the above topics that you have enjoyed the most and explore further possibilities.

CONCLUSION

Whatever the means of communication in our increasingly technological age, the need for, and the use of, letters and alphabets get ever greater. We depend more and more on letters and alphabets so as to express and communicate our ideas, and transmit information to other people.

Society today is far more aware of letter forms in everyday interaction and this is necessarily so at international venues such as conferences and exhibitions, as well as at airports and railway stations, and on the Internet too.

Awareness, therefore, of other languages and alphabets is inevitable. A knowledge of other alphabetic forms is not only a desirable attribute but an increasing necessity. Such knowledge helps to build understanding of, and a more positive insight into, other people's cultures and societies in a shrinking but interdependent world.

Alphabets, whatever their differences, have a lot in common. They are creative forms in their own right and, as such, provide a reassuring basis in which to express artistic endeavour. It is easier to "start off" when building on a familiar and recognisable subject matter, such as an alphabet, when doing your own artwork.

As alphabets share common visual elements, design work based on the different letters helps an artist to see the subject in a familiar as well as in an original way.

Letters are made up of vertical, horizontal and diagonal lines, circles, semi-circles, squares and other geometric forms, and these constituent parts provide a firm basis for design.

There are strong similarities between the Greek, Roman and Cyrillic alphabets and many letters appear exactly the same in all of them. Armenian and Georgian, although rather different, nevertheless lend themselves to artistic design because of their recognisable connection with the Greek alphabet.

In visual education, "the representational crisis" is a very real obstacle in artistic expression especially for children in school. Young people want to record accurately, usually in pencil, as close an approximation to the real thing as possible, whether object, figure or plant.

The person who is unable to record convincingly is "no good at art", and does not want to go on further with the subject. Because everyone is familiar with letters from a very early age, and because letters are largely free of representational likeness, they make a sound and reassuring basis on which students can express themselves. In addition, letters are versatile forms and lend themselves to extraordinary manipulation and development.

A lot of art material in this book created by younger students indicates a strong pictorial approach with a marked preference for pattern work. Emphasis on pattern rather than the other design elements suggests a prior knowledge of letter forms. If this is so, it certainly helps an adolescent to sort out an apparently wide range of design elements. It can help stimulate judgement and a practical approach to design.

Both adults and children tend to pick a letter, or letters, with personal or emotional connotations, the most obvious being the letters that comprise their initials. There is a marked leaning towards angular letters, particularly A, E and M, and where letters are based on the circle or semi-circle such as the letter S, they are often treated in an angular way.

Angular letters convey geometric qualities very well visually, and this allows them to be manipulated in a personal way. The characteristics of a letter or word tend to be selected in such a way as to serve its function. Words with highly charged sensational values in which letters can be instantly distorted so as to emphasize exciting effects such as "stretch", "wriggle", "crash", "flashing", "melt", "panic", "kill", "fight", "smash", are preferred.